G000150849

# 1% The book

# that the financial establishment doesn't want you to read

Copyright © 2019 R.E. Sharratt
Geneva, Switzerland

All rights reserved.

ISBN: 978-1-7943-4194-4

*For those who are willing to take a stand against a dishonest system.*

*Money isn't just about value. It is also about values.*

# CONTENTS

# PREFACE

*"I know of only three people who really understand money."* [1]

J.M. Keynes

The 1% are the 1% because of money and because of their relationship with the banking system.

This is the first book ever that gives a genuine behind-the-curtain look at how banks really function and their impact on society. It reveals that banks create most of the money in an economy, not the state. It shows why inequality and discrimination against out-groups are institutional. It explains how banks are the main contributors to booms and busts in the economy. It shows why central bank monetary policy is largely ineffective. It reveals that, for core banking functions, the banking industry is almost entirely unregulated. It shows that, unlike almost all other industries, the banking sector enjoys unparalleled protection against competition. It suggests potential reforms and an alternative system that could lead to a better world. In the end, this is not really a book about money and banking; it is more about our values as a society.

**What will you get out of this book?**

- This book is designed to help you understand money.

- You need to understand what money is before you can understand the banking system.

- You need to understand the banking system in order to understand the impact of the 1% on society.

- You need to understand the economic drivers of society in order to consider potential reforms or alternatives.

- Money is fundamental to life; you need to evaluate the current banking system based on your values.

---

1 John Maynard Keynes, British economist, cited by several contemporary sources. Unfortunately, for him, Keynes does not appear to be one of these three.

**Who should read this book?**

- People who want to know the source of the 1%'s power.

- People who want to understand how the banking system contributes to inequality.

- People who want to know why there is regular excess variance in the business cycle.

- People who want to make the world a better place.

**This book will help you solve some mysteries, like the following:**

- Why is fractional reserve banking like a distorted version of the game Monopoly?

- Why does the establishment find women's sexual education repugnant?

- Why does the economy blow up from time to time?

- Why was Karl Marx so pissed off?

- What does Professor Sybill Trelawney have in common with the governors of the Federal Reserve?

- Where is the darkest place on Earth, from an economics perspective?

This book solves these mysteries, using straight-forward language.

Most books about money or the 1% are written by academic economists or radical activists. These writers typically have something in common: they have never worked in a bank. They don't understand the inside technical details. Other commentators are only really familiar with financial markets, which do not involve money creation.

In this case, the author is a former banker. He has experience of making loans, building financial models, coding risk algorithms, and the management accounting used inside banks. This book reveals details of the banking process that have never been made public.

# 1

# WHAT THE 1% KNOWS THAT YOU DON'T

If you really want to understand the 1%, guess where you need to start? That's right: money. This book is written in simple language, because the 1% are hoping that complexity will prevent you from learning the truth about the source of their power. Here is the background you need to know.

The story of money is the story of human evolution.

Our ancient ancestors' development of money was driven by our *biology* and our *values*. The history of money can be separated into two parts:

A period where money had an explicit link to value. This period existed from the dawn of money in Neolithic times, as humans started to cultivate crops and domesticate animals, and lasted for most of the rest of human history.

A recent period, where this explicit link has been broken. This period followed the rise of precious metal depositories (the forerunners of modern banks).

**Money arose, essentially, as an extension of memory.**

As our ancestors evolved, they assumed increasingly specialised roles in society. Some might concentrate on making footwear, others to tending livestock, others in raising crops. Money represented *the concept of value created through specialised effort*, which was used by the group and then, later, exchanged with others through trade. Small groups remembered that the makers of footwear had done their part earlier, when the meat came in froma hunt. We acquired the concept of stored memory to shift value across time periods. Between groups we learned to exchange valuable items, either at the same time or with one group giving food now in return for a promise to receive food in the future from the other group. As we specialised further and

1

repeated exchanges across time, this gradually led to the concept of a standard of value, as barter exchange became too complex for us to remember. This was the first step towards money and a standard of value for exchange existed amongst communities in Mesopotamia and along the Nile River by ~3,000 BC. [2]

**A standard of value was necessary before any other aspects of money could emerge.**

Exchanges of valuable items needed to be comparable and many societies used what was most available, such as wheat or barley. [3] In Ancient Rome, cattle (*pecus*) become a standard of value, from which we get the word pecuniary. These standards of value also had other rudimentary, secondary characteristics useful for money: they are (somewhat) divisible, portable, durable, etc. and also their supply is naturally limited.

Due to the rarity of double coincidence of wants, barter probably never really existed outside of small groups that didn't want for much. As human groups became larger, people conceived of value in relation to a common standard (like barley); this allowed the emergence of a *medium of exchange.* So, a goat herder could sell a goat to a shoemaker, even if he already had enough shoes; the shoemaker could simply pay in barley. The goat would be valued according to a standard of value, measured in barley. Even if the goat herder didn't want barley he could accept it as payment, as he knew that he could use the barley as a way to buy something else he wanted. Barley also allowed him to buy a variety of items or to spend some now and keep the rest for future purchases.

Any medium of exchange implies that the item is also *a store of value*, otherwise it would not be accepted in exchange. Barley is a store of value, as no one can magically create a huge supply of barley. A national currency that is subject to inflation is a poor store of value, as it is worth less every day; therefore, it is a poor medium of exchange (because who would really choose it, if it is constantly declining in value?).

2 P. Einzig, *Primitive Money: In its Ethnological, Historical and Economic Aspects*, 2nd edn., London, Pergamon Press, 1966. M. Powell, 'Money in Mesopotamia', *Journal of the Economic and Social History of the Orient*, vol. 39, no. 3, 1996, pp. 224-242.

3 Amongst the earliest recorded civilisations to use money were the Sumerians. By the time they codified a standard of value, this was still expressed in barley, although silver had become the main medium of exchange. R.F. Harper, *The Code of Hammurabi*, Chicago, 1904, p. 37. S. Homer and R. Sylla, *A History of Interest Rates*, 4th edn., Hoboken, John Wiley & Sons, 2005.

**Through a process of evolution, our ancestors developed the concept of money.**

Essentially, money reflects *the memory of something valuable that was created by our efforts*, like raising livestock or making shoes. It allowed us to specialise and exchange items of value, so we were all better off. Money is often defined using complex language, but it only has two, simple, common-sense characteristics:

1. Money needs to be scarce.

2. Money needs to be accepted by others as having purchasing power.

**Money co-evolved with our understanding of sacrifice.**

Humans gradually learned that sacrifice today could mean more of something tomorrow. Some of our earliest writing dealt with loans from those who had surplus grains to those who presumably had the ability and inclination to put the grains to productive use. Seeds planted today, rather than eaten with a crop, could mean more next season. Borrowers could repay lenders from what was brought forth by their efforts: when the grain harvest was brought in, a certain percentage was given to those who had sacrificed. Loans and interest due were recorded on tablets and quoted in money [4]; this usually happened at temples, which were principal meeting places for the community. [5] Many societies set limits on interest rates, had rules for times when the harvest failed, etc. [6] Sacrifice, a form of savings, and productive use of the savings, benefited both parties. A primitive economy grew bigger: more land was brought under cultivation, more animals were raised. Savings (sacrifice), recorded as a form of money, led to a better existence for humanity.

**Money itself has no intrinsic value.**

Gold, US dollars, bitcoin, etc. have value only to the extent that they are scarce and are commonly accepted to purchase goods and services. Money is a

---

4 Einzig, *op. cit.*, p. 206.

5 This was almost always the case in Sumer and Mesopotamia. In Ancient Rome, the Roman treasury was historically in the temple of Juno Monetas, the goddess of memory; this is where Roman coins were minted. The temple was also the place where the official ledgers of the magistrates were stored. Monere is the Latin word meaning to remind (admonere) or to warn. From Monetas we get the word for money.

6 Homer and Sylla, *op. cit.*

*symbol*, a representation of purchasing power; it is not valuable in itself.[7] If aliens show up tomorrow and want to sell us a cure for cancer, they are unlikely to take gold bars in payment. Undoubtedly, their home planet also has the element Au (gold), caused by the explosion of neutron stars a few billion years ago, and they are not likely to value it very much. Probably they would find it amusing that we spend time digging up, refining and then guarding gold. They might think that if we didn't waste our time like this, we might have discovered a cure for cancer ourselves.

**Since money has no intrinsic value, it must be trusted.**

When you create something of value (for example, by making shoes, or selling your time to your employer), you need to trust the money you get in return for your effort. You need to trust that what you are getting in exchange will give you the ability to purchase things, now or in the future. The basis of all good money is trust, just as it is the basis for all good human relationships.

**Precious metals emerged as the global money in many places.**

Where precious metals were present geologically most societies adopted them as money.[8] Why did this happen, in an uncoordinated manner, around the world? Most importantly, because precious metals are scarce. This allows something that has no intrinsic value to act as a symbol that retains purchasing power over time.[9] This led to groups of people accepting that precious metals represented a store of value, which could be used as exchange for goods or services in ever distant trade. So, by definition, they had purchasing power; their common acceptance was a benefit for the real economy. The global acceptance of precious metals meant that their value was not tied to the actions of specific nation states.

Precious metals had other, common-sense characteristics as a representation of value: they lasted a long time, were hard to damage, could be divided into smaller units, each unit had the same value as any other, etc. Their value was

7 Some items were used as money that have value in themselves, like barley or cigarettes, but, when used for an exchange purpose, their value was their scarcity and purchasing power, not because you could eat or smoke them. If the goat seller, for example, just wanted to buy barley, he probably would not have gone to the shoemaker.

8 The earliest form of precious metal money in Mesopotamia was originally copper. In Ancient Rome it was the *aes rude*, which was copper or bronze. In Indonesia, tin was used in trade and Sparta used iron. Eventually, gold and silver became more prominent. Einzig, *op. cit.*

9 Precious metals did not have consistent global pricing until the emergence of modern logistics, but acceptance of precious metals by diverse civilisations facilitated exchange amongst groups and, eventually, nations. In many ways, gold and silver were a global money for most of human history: they were scarce and they were accepted as having purchasing power.

based on their weight. Eventually, probably in Lydia [10], precious metals were made into standard units called coins, to facilitate commerce. Since they come from distant, exploded stars, precious metals are rather hard to counterfeit. In addition, primitive humans, unlike us today, probably used gold and silver because they liked shiny things with a bit of bling to them.

**Precious metal depositories led to the creation of modern banks. It was the end of an era for what our ancestors would have considered "money".**

Gold and silver were concentrated in the hands of governments and guilds, who acted as producers, issuers, and depositories. As carrying gold and silver around was sometimes inconvenient and risky, precious metal depositories issued paper IOUs to their customers, depositors like merchants. These paper IOUs, backed by the value of precious metal, could be used as a more convenient form of making purchases; the IOUs themselves began to circulate as a form of money. The depositories learned that not all customers demanded access to their gold or silver at the same time. This presented *an opportunity to make loans using paper receipts* for more than the total amount of precious metal that they physically held. In this way a "fraction" of the value was kept in reserve and the rest could be lent out to borrowers. [11]

Borrowers, doing something productive in the real economy, had an obligation to repay the lender a greater amount than was lent to them, secured against their real economy assets. This allowed the depository to earn a significant lending profit from each reserve amount. Of course, there was a risk as well: what if all customers came in and wanted their gold back?

However, the real risk to the depository was relatively low: obligations were covered either by gold in storage or by real asset collateral. As further security, loans were also backed by the expected future cashflows of the productive use of the lent "money". What became crucial was not the gold on deposit, but rather the confidence that users had in the depository. This confidence made the difference between a successful and an unsuccessful depository, not the ability of users to see how much gold really existed behind the scenes. Modern banks use *exactly the same model* as the depositories from history.

---

10 From the Greek historian, Herodotus, *The Histories*. R. Cook, 'Speculations on the Origin of Coinage', *Historia*, vol. 7, no. 3, 1958, pp. 257-262.

11 This is double spending: the depository had gold on deposit from the customer and, at the same time, lent some of this gold to a borrower. The original gold is the only representation of value created in the real economy. Actually, depositories (banks) spend much more than twice. A 10% fractional reserve ratio means that ~9x the original "value" deposit is created in paper IOU money, in purchasing power.

If you want to understand the roots of inequality and solve the greatest mystery in modern economics, the cancer that is the extreme variance [12] in the business cycle that metastasises every 1-2 decades, here is the question to ask:

*Are the gold and the IOUs the same thing?*

We know that no money has any intrinsic value. The gold is a symbolic representation, a token, that represents value. The IOU is a token on a token. They both have purchasing power. So, is there any difference between them? This is the question that the 1%, the financial elite, don't want you to ask. The answer to this seemingly obscure, technical question from history is why they are rich. And, why you are not. It is the basis for why the banking system inherently favours in-groups and discriminates against out-groups. It is the basis for inequality in society.

The question seems so innocent. Yet, the impact of the answer on society is profound. Let's see if we can solve this mystery.

---

12 Of course, some volatility is to be expected and at certain amount does, in fact, provide valuable information to participants in the economy. A natural amount of volatility is beneficial to the economy, as it gets rid of dead wood and makes the overall system stronger. Here, we refer to excess variance, the exponential effect of bank credit money on a natural process and also its abnormal impact on asset pricing.

**Money and banking are inextricably linked.**

The history of money can be broadly divided into two periods, as set out below.

| Time period | Money | Banking |
|---|---|---|
| From the time early humans began to specialise, sacrifice, and to exchange value, until the rise of precious metal depositories. | All money represented *value already created*, by productive effort in the real economy. This is present value (**PV**) money. | The banking function matched surplus capital (e.g. grain, gold) to productive opportunities in the economy. |
| From the establishment of these depositories (eventually called banks) [13] until the present day. | Two forms of money begin to exist, side by side: (1) PV money. For example, gold coins. (2) Future value (**FV**) money, where the value was *linked to an expected future cashflow* stream, which didn't exist currently (at the time that the FV money was created). An example is paper IOUs or promise to pay bearer notes. | Banking matched PV money (e.g. gold) to productive opportunities. It _also_ began to evolve into issuing paper IOUs in return for future cashflows from productive opportunities, in the form of loans. As both gold and IOUs were relatively scarce and were accepted as having purchasing power, *two types of money existed* side by side: PV money (value already created; <u>no credit risk</u> in exchange) and FV money (value expected to be created in the future; those who accept it take <u>credit risk</u> on the issuer). [14] |

13 Bank comes from the Italian word for bench. The term originated in Venice, where money lenders would do their business with borrowers while seated on benches. Of course, the gold, the representation of value and purchasing power, was kept elsewhere, secure in vaults, themselves behind curtains. If the IOUs are accepted as having purchasing power, who cares about seeing the actual gold? Today, in Italian, the same word is used to refer to a bench and a bank (with different meanings, of course).

14 Understanding which money involves taking credit risk (FV money) and which does not (PV money) is one of the first steps to understanding bank created credit money, the power that fuels the 1%. It is also the foundation of understanding excess variance in the business cycle.

Although this was an evolution, it led to a decisive change in what money meant to humanity:

*The rise of modern banking broke the historic link to when money represented the memory of something valuable created.*

## Takeaways

1. A bank's ability to make a loan also means that it can create its own version of money (the IOU). It has purchasing power, just like government-issued money.
2. Once issued, the two are indistinguishable from each other (to you). But, this bank money has something special about it, something dark, which we are going to discover.
3. Banks use this money-creating ability to advance their own interests and sustain related parties.
4. The 1% exerts a significant influence on society mainly through money and the banking system.
5. The 1% don't want you to understand how money and the banking system work, especially that they can create their own money.

## Who cares?

You do. Money is power. [15] The ability to create money is a controlling power in a society. This power is in the hands of the government and the banks. Read that again, so it sinks in. Money is power. And dominance. And the banks create their own money. Which they use for their own objectives. And the objectives of the 1%. And those who enable them. You are at the tip of the iceberg in terms of understanding the 1% and their influence. Money creation, the power, the inequality in society, the booms and the busts in the economy; the key to understanding is hidden behind the technical complexity of something that seems so simple: money. It takes effort to understand money and banking. But, it is all written in this book, in as simple terms as possible, if you are willing to make the effort.

Here are some good concomitant questions: How much money do banks create compared to the government? What constraints exist on the banks' ability to create money? How is this regulated? Is this money creation disclosed anywhere? If not, why not? Let's find out.

---

15 OK, that is such a banal statement that I feel a little embarrassed writing it. But, you asked.

## Neolithic man comes up with the idea of banking

# 2
# THE SOURCE OF THE 1%'S MONEY

To understand where the 1% get their money from, *you need to understand more about banks*. I know, it's a bit boring. Some people prefer to sit around and play video games or watch your favourite sports team or spend time on social media. That is what the 1% are counting on.

For those of you who want to live a better life, and make the world a better place, please keep reading. As an incentive, there are sections on sex and on drinking later in the book. Well, from an economics perspective.

**How banks make loans.**

Banks are simply investment companies. They evaluate a potential investment (the loan) based on risk and return, the basis of modern finance theory since Harry Markowitz in the 1950s, just like other actors in the economy. There is something special about banks, though; if you keep reading you will be one of the few who really understand banks and money.

First, here is how bank lending works.

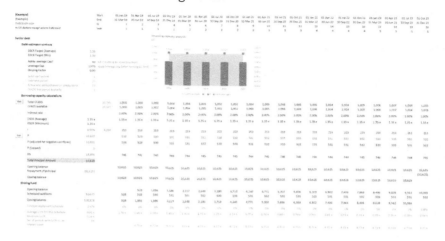

OK, so what should you pay attention to here? Look at the CFADS number. That stands for Cash Flow Available for Debt Service and it is a standard acronym used by bank insiders. The calculation is set out below.

|  | Operating profit |
|---|---|
| *add back* | non-cash expenses (e.g. accounting depreciation) |
| *minus* | cash taxes to be paid [16] |
| *adjust for* | changes in net working capital |
| *minus* | capital expenditure (basic, or maintenance, capex) |
| *equals* | CFADS |

Don't really care? Well, think of it as the main ingredient that goes into how banks create money. It is crucial to understanding a part of how the 1% finances itself, using some of your money. And, it is the building block to understanding why our economy blows up every now and then.

Banks forecast CFADS using qualitative factors (like the competitive position of a company in its industry) and quantitative factors (like historical performance and expected growth of the economy).

The example above shows an actual commercial bank lending model. It illustrates how a bank estimates the principal amount a company could

---

16 Even though CFADS is before debt interest tax shields, which impact on tax payable, banks adjust for taxes to be paid. It is a bit of a circularity, but this is the standard approach.

borrow for a 5-year senior debt loan with a bullet repayment (meaning, the amount borrowed is repaid at the end of year 5; in the meantime, the borrower pays interest, on a quarterly basis). [17] These kind of models are one of many internal processes that banks don't want you to know about.

The loan officer determines a debt service coverage ratio (DSCR), which is the amount of "headroom" the expected cashflow will cover the amount that the company needs to repay each period. The loan officer also selects the interest rate on the loan. Both are set in relation to the perceived credit risk of the borrower.

Based on the amount of expected cashflow, the interest rate and the amount of headroom, the principal amount of the loan is calculated. [18] In this example, the maximum principal amount that could be borrowed is $10,625. Total repayments (principal and interest) are $14,875. The difference is interest (profit) to the bank: $4,250.

Sophisticated banks don't just use a single input in the CFADS formula. Instead, they use a statistical model for forecasting, based on a distribution range of potential inputs. [19]

If you are cynical, you might think that your average loan officer probably doesn't do this. It is true that loan officers are human and humans are sometimes lazy. This kind of loan evaluation is complex and is only done, by definition, for loans that are expected to bring in future cashflows. [20]

There are other options for loan officers who want to be on the golf course by 3 pm: they can make consumer loans or asset loans, which are simpler. They also, consciously or subconsciously, use heuristics in decision-making.

---

17 The other repayment option is a declining balance (mortgage) style loan, where some of the principal amount gets repaid each period. Bullet repayment loans may have a sinking fund attached to them. The type of loan and these mechanics are not important for our thesis.

18 This is a simplified example. There are a few other considerations, but they don't have much impact and don't change the thesis. The calculation of the principal amount is done by an algorithm written in computer code; the output is shown here.

19 This model uses @Risk statistical modelling software to apply a distribution shape to inputs; you just see the expected output for CFADS.

20 This includes balance sheet loans, where a bank lends against a general corporate obligation to repay. In this case, sometimes banks may not explicitly control the use of funds. However, good bank loan documents are detailed, with covenant tests, and they usually don't allow you to use the money to go to the casino and put it all on black.

A few biases in the lending process are set out below.

1.   Banking is all about trust. Humans, including bank loan officers, instinctively have greater trust in people who are similar to them. Consequently, banks are more likely to make loans (especially with attractive terms) to in-groups, rather than out-groups, based on similarity between lender and borrower. Preferences are incorporated into the DSCR.

2.   Employees of large organisations, like banks, are mainly motivated by preserving their jobs. Consequently, they are more likely to make loans to low perceived controversy borrowers (e.g. based on name recognition, history with the bank, people their boss likes) than higher perceived controversy borrowers (e.g. smaller, newer borrowers or borrowers that may be lower risk, but require individual reputational risk from the loan officer).

**There are three broad uses of funds from a bank loan. Two have to do with future cashflows. The third is the cause of most business cycle excess variance.**

In general, there are three areas to which banks make loans, which are set out below.

| Loan use | Example | Effort level for the bank loan officer | Risk to the bank loan officer of getting fired if things go wrong | Repayment |
|---|---|---|---|---|
| **1. Productive economic activities** | Buy new equipment, hire people to expand output. | High. God, I have to come up with all of those numbers to input into the financial model again. Then, I have to go to the credit committee. | Medium. A lot of model inputs could turn out to be wrong. "It is tough to make predictions, especially about the future." Yogi Berra. | Company sells stuff that people want to buy. Future cashflow stream. |
| **2. Time shifting of income/ Consumer consumption** | A mortgage, or you want to "bring forward" some of your future salary to go on a vacation now. | Low. Check salary statements, get asset valuation from third party, if needed. | Low. Run standard bank policies. | Customer keeps getting a salary. Future cashflow stream. |
| **3. Asset purchases** | Someone uses a bank loan to finance a real estate investment or to buy stocks. | Low. Get asset valuation (usually a market price, from a third party, or check bank policy). | Very low. Bank policy on securities lending. Or, bricks and mortar lending; what could go wrong? | Future sale of the asset, at a higher price that it was purchased for. [21] No/little future cashflow stream. [22] |

21 Otherwise, there is no/not enough future cashflow stream to support the loan. Want a loan to buy a stock, a piece of art, land on which to build some real estate? Great, our bank loves lending to tangible assets. However, if you don't eventually sell it at a higher price to someone else then, unlike other loans, you cannot squeeze the art to get cashflow out of it when it comes time to repay. This is the principle of loans for asset purchases. Want to understand excess variance in business cycles? Well, *keep your eyes on asset loans.*

22 Yes, in some asset loans there are minor cashflow repayment means, like dividends from stock purchases or rent from commercial real estate. However, these are usually insignificant when it

For asset lending, you may be thinking to yourself, "wow, some banks use poor suckers' money in the hope that asset prices will go up. Glad that isn't what my money is being used for." [23] If this is what you are thinking, now would be a good point for you to stop reading. [24]

## Where did the "money" come from for the loan?

The sources of funds (the money) for the bank to make loans are set out below.

1. Savings (i.e. deposits or rather, technically, loans, from people like you).

2. Their own funds (i.e. profits that they make and retain in the bank).

3. Borrowings (either from the central bank, interbank market, or bond issues).

4. Their own, internal credit money creation.

The first three sources (savings, own funds, borrowings) are lent out in part, but they make up a minority of bank lending. [25] The majority comes from creating "credit money". How it works is simple and is set out below.

Let's use our example from above. Say that the bank decides to go ahead and loan a company the principal amount that they calculated: $10,625. The risk and return characteristics seem acceptable. The bank will give you $10,625 today, in return for $14,875 in the future (over the next 5 years). That is an 8% per year return. What is their cost of funds? Well, for the first three sources, it

---

comes to the size of debt repayment. Further, in an economic downturn, stocks pay less dividends and commercial rents decline; for the bank, the security is in the asset value. Debt repayment is based on the asset value, using so-called "loan to value" (LTV) ratios. What is value? Well, *for asset loans, keep your eyes on what mechanism is used to determine value.* That is a big part of the solution to the mystery.

23 Or, at least hope that the asset won't decline in value.

24 You also need to stop lying to yourself and accept: it isn't your money. The money you have in your deposit account isn't yours and isn't a deposit. Legally, it is an unsecured loan from you to the bank. Recall that our modern banks grew out of precious metal depositories. Calling it a Deposit Account is also a little better marketing than calling it an Unsecured Loan to Us Account. If your bank gets into trouble, then you are an unsecured creditor of the bank; you have no other claim to your money. Probably there is some bank insurance in your country, so maybe the government will pay you back, since they can just print "money" (who cares if it doesn't purchase the same amount of stuff?). These fears are what led to bank runs in the past. Don't think that bank runs exist anymore? Maybe you are not old enough to remember the 2008 financial crisis. That was a modern bank run, cleverly disguised. Don't worry if you have forgotten, it will happen again.

25 Most of these funds are used for the banks own reserve capital, sometimes held with the central bank; some also supports correspondent bank accounts (the bank's own accounts with other banks). Correspondent accounts are how banks and national banking systems link to each other. This is how payments happen. Another way to think of correspondent accounts amongst banks is how excess business cycle variance is transmitted throughout the financial system. If you are scientifically minded, you can think of these inter-linked bank accounts as similar to how viruses spread.

is low. As the saver (unsecured lender to the bank, really, but let's keep up the charade for the example), what do you get in interest on your bank account? What do you think the central bank charges them? Right, not very much.

OK, but if most of these funds come from their own internal money creation, what is the cost of this? The answer is *not very much*. The main costs to the bank are related to having other banks accept your newly created credit money. As with everything in banking and money, the key issue is *confidence*. In a fractional reserve banking system, it is obvious that if everyone loses trust in your bank, it will fail. There are never enough reserves (real, PV money) to pay back all depositors. Confidence-related economic costs are: advertising (to create brand image), payments to central banks, transfers to the political sector, etc. The biggest economic cost to any bank is related to the confidence amongst users that it will be there tomorrow. More confidence = lower cost of funding.

Modern banking, like the precious metal depositories, is all about the *illusion* of stability. You must give the impression that the gold is all there. Your money is sitting here in your account with your name on it, don't worry. One way to preserve the illusion is to attack any questioners as too ignorant, too stupid to understand banking.

Internally, banks work out their cost of funding for loans using the following simple formula:

$$= w_t \cdot savings_t + w_t \cdot own\ funds_t + w_t \cdot borrowings_t + w_t \cdot credit\ money_t$$

This is just the weighted average of the sources of funds. In the example, the weighted cost of funds for the bank is just less than 2%. So, the expected economic profit for the bank is about 6%, or 3/4ths of the interest rate charged. This relative profit percentage is typical for corporate lending; it is lower for larger borrowers and higher for smaller borrowers. For consumer lending, the profit percentages are typically higher than corporate.

The accounting for this newly created credit money is based on double-entry (matched) bookkeeping, like all accounting, and is as set out below.

The loan of $10,625 is an *asset* to the bank, since the company will pay them $10,625 in future cashflows (hopefully). This is entered on their ledger, their balance sheet, in the assets column. The bank now has to give the loan money to the company; this is a *liability* to them. They do this by creating a deposit account in the amount of $10,625. [26] This is FV money; its value is matched to

---

26 This is a liability of the bank to the company (i.e. to pay them "money") and is exactly the same as

the loan, which is (hopefully) going to come in via future cashflows. There is no real-world value created today, as our ancestors in the Liberty Tribe in the cartoon knew. There is an asset (the loan), which is based on an obligation for future payments by the company, but this asset isn't "real" yet; its value hasn't materialised at the time that the asset is created.

Note that the money in the borrower's deposit account looks exactly the same as a PV deposit of value, but there are some differences. For one, the use of funds is restricted. The borrower needs to use it for the purposes that they declared to get the loan. This falls into the three categories that we discussed:

1.  to invest in productive purposes to make stuff that people want to buy,

2.  to time-shift consumption, and

3.  to invest in an asset in the belief that it will increase in value.

Banks are intentionally *opaque* and hard to understand. If you were an outsider, not part of the guild (for example, if you were an economist or a consultant in your ivory tower), and you looked at the balance sheet or read aggregated national statistics, you might think that the deposit is just money from savers that has been matched to a loan. You wouldn't be totally wrong, just almost totally wrong. A small portion of the weighted sources of funds does typically come from savings and the cost of savings does factor into the cost of lending. This what banks and their enablers want you to believe: that they just helpfully match savings with borrowings.

**You don't just need to believe me. Here is some evidence.**

Don't believe that commercial banks create money? Well, how about asking some central banks themselves? In the United Kingdom, according to an obscure report in their in-house journal, the Bank of England states that 97% of the money supply comes from credit money creation by commercial banks.[27] In Germany, according to the Bundesbank, the vast majority of money

---

the deposit account that you have at a bank. Your deposit account is where your salary is paid into each month. Wait a minute, you might be thinking, I have already worked for this money in my deposit account; I sold my time to my employer. So, "my" "money" should be seen as PV money. Value has already been created in the economy. Hmmm, maybe this has something to do with the greatest mystery in economics thing ...

27 M. McLeay et al., 'Money Creation in the Modern Economy', *Bank of England Quarterly Bulletin*, Q1, 2014. The BoE actually obfuscates the issue: it has other papers that state that banks are financial intermediaries and also some papers that make reference to the money multiplier effect.

is created by commercial banks.[28] In Switzerland, it is about 90%.[29] Guess what it is in the United States?[30] The percentage varies over time, but it is broadly above 90% in advanced economies.

Is this news to you, that banks create most of the "money" in an economy? Well, don't feel silly; the banks don't want you to know this. Switzerland is one of the most financially literate countries in the world, with one of the highest GDPs per capita, home to one-third of global offshore wealth.[31] Yet, even here only 13% of respondents in a recent poll knew that banks created most of the money in Switzerland. This seems strange, as we all use money every day and it is so central to our lives. If you asked Swiss people where cheese comes from, most could probably identify cows as the main source. In earlier eras of our history, humans could probably tell you where, say, coins came from. Why so different today? Why such a mystery?

In the event that you ever took a course in economics at university, there is a reason why you don't know that commercial banks create the vast majority of the money supply: you have been lied to. As an example, Gregory Mankiw's *Macroeconomics*, the most widely used introductory textbook in the United States, continues a falsehood first perpetrated by Paul Samuelson's textbook in 1948. These textbooks teach that only the national government creates money, as well as the money multiplier theory of money creation; they do not reveal that banks create credit money themselves, through their own loan process.[32] Standard economics textbooks teach that banks lend out existing deposits. They state that the collective actions of the banking system then can create some additional money supply, as loans from one bank then become deposits of other banks, up until a ceiling imposed by a central bank (called the reserve requirement). So, in textbooks, the reserve requirement is crucial to the amount of money in an economy and banks don't create money themselves.

Here is a little science experiment. Textbooks teach that money is created

28 The role of banks, non-banks and the central bank in the money creation process'. *Deutsche Bundesbank Publications*, vol. 69, no. 4, 2017, pp. 13-34.

29 Dr Emma Dawnay, *Vollgeld Initiative*, 2016.

30 Just joking. In the United States, the land of the free, their government and banks do not reveal this information to their citizens. In fact, their education system teaches that banks are simple intermediaries between savers and borrowers and do not create money.

31 BCG Global Wealth Report, 2018.

32 So, it is a little embarrassing when other central banks, like the Bank of England, actually state clearly that, no, central banks don't create most of the money supply. Most of the money supply comes from commercial banks in an economy by making loans. But, the textbooks never change, never reveal the truth about money creation, even when central banks themselves state it clearly. Why could that be?

collectively by the banking system, controlled by a money multiplier, imposed by the central bank's reserve requirement. So, a reserve requirement is a necessary component of money creation, right? Well, what about countries like Canada, Australia, the United Kingdom, Sweden, etc. where there is no reserve requirement? How do the textbooks explain that? Well, they can't. Regardless, empirically, there is a weak correlation between reserve requirements (where they do exist, like in the United States) and money creation in an economy. Similarly, there is a weak correlation between savings and money creation. [33]

You may be asking yourself: if changes in the money supply (which impact inflation and cause excess variance in the business cycle, both bad news) don't really come from savings or from this money multiplier concept, then how does this impact bank regulation? If banks create the vast majority of money in an economy and they do it by themselves, based mainly on their own estimates of future value, how are they regulated? We are going to get to that in a minute. As advance warning, you probably don't want to know.

An even more ridiculous theory taught in economics classes is that banks are just financial intermediaries and that they don't create money; this theory states that only the national government creates money. This theory is taught alongside the money multiplier/fractional reserve model mentioned above. Banks are just simply channeling savings to productive use. So nice and helpful of them. Here is an interesting quote about why this quite misleading information is taught to the public, from an economist who wasn't afraid of telling the truth.

*"The study of money, above all other fields in economics, is one in which complexity is used to disguise truth or to evade truth, not to reveal it. The process by which banks create money is so simple the mind is repelled. With something so important, a deeper mystery seems only decent."*[34] JOHN KENNETH GALBRAITH.

The only significant living economist who has actually done an honest, empirical investigation into the mechanics of bank money creation, who has really gotten his hands dirty evaluating actual banking work, is Dr Richard Werner, a professor in the UK with a doctorate from Oxford. [35] He has

---

33 You can measure total savings (which would be incorrect) or available savings depending on changes in the interest rate paid on savings deposits; it doesn't matter. Both correlations are weak.

34 J. Galbraith, *Money: Whence it came, where it went*, Princeton University Press, 1975, p.22.

35 He isn't a banker and he doesn't get into the workings that you would know if you were an insider, but he actually did field research!! It is incredible, as the biggest sin in being an economics professor

compared scientifically the three main theories of money creation (money multiplier, banks as intermediaries, and credit money creation). [36] He is able to disprove the two standard theories taught in economics: the money multiplier and banks as intermediaries. They are demonstrably false. The credit money creation theory matches with what banks actually do in the real economy and cannot be disproved.

Yet, despite this, most well-known economists still continue to support theories that are disproved by evidence and by admissions from central banks themselves. Why is that? There are a few reasons, including: mainstream economists don't include banks and money very much in their explanations for how the overall economy works; they are so wedded to their axioms of banks as neutral agents in an economy, simply allocating capital, that, intellectually, it requires an exceptionally strong effort to be genuinely self-critical of what you have learned; not a single one of them has actually worked as a banker, as far as I can find [37]; and, the vast majority, directly or indirectly, benefit financially from continuing to support the party line and avoiding biting the hand that feeds them. For others, in a world where you can see that the emperor has no clothes on, it takes a lot of guts to speak up and tell the truth. Guilds and their enablers don't change from the inside.

In fact, like most things to do with modern banking, the situation isn't black and white. There is a (small) element of the truth in banks acting as financial intermediaries and fractional reserve/the money multiplier does play a role in money creation. However, the vast majority of money creation comes from the banks' own credit processes. What the banking industry and their enablers do, however, is point to the (relatively) less harmful theories (intermediaries, money multiplier effect of the system), while intentionally remaining silent about the largest contributor: that individual banks create FV money through the lending process, which is then co- mingled with PV money (money where the value has already been created) so that the two "monies" are indistinguishable from each other.

---

seems to be actually applying your trade, getting your hands dirty with commerce. You won't find that with any Nobel prize winners.

36 R. Werner, 'A Lost century in economics: Three theories of banking and the conclusive evidence', *International Review of Financial Analysis*, vol. 46, pp. 361-379.

37 Economics is one of the few professions where you can be an expert without ever having worked in your area of expertise. I mean, if you want to be a golf pro, it helps if you have swung a golf club. Not so with economists who "teach" about banking. Yet, when these same economists go to the doctor, you can be pretty sure that they select someone who has real experience, not just someone who has read about how medicine works and has developed grand theories.

**Does bank credit money come from nothing? Is it created by the stroke of a pen?**

It is sometimes suggested that banks can create credit money out of thin air. This idea can, perhaps, be dated to a comment from one of the founders of the Bank of England: "*The bank hath benefit of interest on all moneys which it creates out of nothing.*" [38] The phrase "out of nothing" sounds very common, so economists translate it into Latin to make it sound better: *ex nihilo.*

Some brilliant minds have repeated this. Niall Ferguson mentions this in *Ascent of Money*. Ray Daglio does the same in his video *How the Economic Machine Works.*

However, *this isn't correct.* Banks don't create credit money from nothing, with the stoke of a pen. It is quite close to being true, though. The reason that most people cannot believe it, and why most economists therefore have not been able to accept the credit money creation theory, is that it just sounds silly. Probably, instinctively, something based on common-sense inside you says: something from nothing isn't very likely. You cannot create gold from nothing.

However, what banks create isn't gold.
It is the IOU.

Formerly, this IOU was linked to gold, to a memory of value created by effort in the past. Today, it is linked to a loan asset, which is expected to bring in a *future* revenue stream. Really, banks are *monetisation entities*. By granting loans-deposit accounts to borrowers, they give them purchasing power today in return for repayment tomorrow. The ratio of:

deposit money created today (equal to the loan amount)
to the expected future cashflows to be received by the bank (adjusted for funding cost, use of funds risk and expected economic performance)

is the most appropriate way of evaluating the risk of bank lending, similar to the Sharpe ratio. [39] There is a noticeable difference in this ratio depending on the use of funds for the loan. The two loan categories related to future

---

38 William Paterson, founder of the Bank of England, from contemporary sources, 1694.

39 This is how central banks or regulators should evaluate the genuine riskiness of banks. Not a single regulator currently does this. Why not? What a mystery. It would require banks individually to reveal how much money they create. Do you think the banks want you to know this information? Can you imagine the regulatory filing? Like: here at JP Morgan we created $x billion of money last quarter, of which x% went into the financing of speculative asset purchases. Henry Ford knew what the public reaction would be, as we will see.

cashflows (productive investment, time shifting) are significantly less risky than asset loans (which are not supported by expected future cashflows).

So, no; credit money doesn't come from nothing or from the stroke of a pen. The foundation for this money comes in large measure from deposits, from hard-working members of the lower and middle class who trust banks with their money. From this money (deposits + bank-created money), banks make substantial lending profits. Depositors earn little on their savings, much less than they are owed based on their contribution and on the risk that they assume. These unjustified margins are the mechanism that channels profits from the many to the 1%.

**Here are some of the few who knew where the 1% gets their money.**

Most people don't see the reality of how money is created. Others see but seek to mislead. Here are some quotes from those who see.

*"If the American people ever allow private banks to control the issue of their currency ... the banks ... will deprive the people of all property until their children wake-up homeless on the continent their fathers conquered .... The issuing power should be taken from the banks and restored to the people, to whom it properly belongs."* [40]
THOMAS JEFFERSON

*"A great industrial nation is controlled by its system of credit. Our system of credit is concentrated in the hands of a few men. We have come to be one of the worst ruled, one of the most completely controlled and dominated governments in the world – no longer a government of free opinion, no longer a government by conviction and vote of the majority, but a government by the opinion and duress of small groups of dominant men."* [41]
WOODROW WILSON

*" It is well enough that people of the nation do not understand our banking and money system, for if they did, I believe there would be a revolution before tomorrow morning."* [42]
HENRY FORD

40 Quoted by contemporaries. Letter to John Taylor, 1816. Letter to John Wayles Eppes, 1813.

41 W. Wilson, *The New Freedom*, New York, Doubleday, Page & Co., 1913. Also quoted by contemporaries.

42 H. Ford and S. Crowther, *My Life and Work*, New York, Doubleday, Page & Co., 1922. Also quoted by contemporaries.

*"Thus, our national circulating medium is now at the mercy of loan transactions of banks, which lend, not money, but promises to supply money they do not possess."*[43]
IRVING FISHER

*"In the absence of the gold standard, there is no way to protect savings from confiscation through inflation. There is no safe store of value. Deficit spending is simply a scheme for the 'hidden' confiscation of wealth."*[44]
ALAN GREENSPAN

## Takeaways

1. Commercial banks create their own money, which is used disproportionately by in-groups (especially, the 1%).
2. This money has purchasing power and is indistinguishable from a real deposit of value into a bank account.
3. This money isn't created out of thin air; it is created based on the banking charter granted by the state and is sustained by confidence in the bank.
4. Most of the money creation power in an economy exists in the banking sector, which creates money based on their views of their own profit potential.
5. The fundamentals of investing (making loans) for a bank means that they structurally prefer in-groups to out-groups.
6. Banks use depositors' funds as part of the money creation process, which leads to substantial profits for banks. Depositors are vastly undercompensated for their contribution to bank profits. This leads to an in-built wealth transfer mechanism from the 99% to the 1%.
7. In no country is this power to create money directly regulated. Nor is the use of these created funds regulated at all.

43 I. Fischer, '100% Money and the Public Debt', *Economic Forum*, April - June 1936, pp. 406-420.
44 A. Greenspan, 'Gold and Economic Freedom', *Objectivist* newsletter, 1966.

# 3
# THE GULF INVESTOR DECEPTION

Nothing illustrates the fact that ~~the 1%~~ banks can create their own credit money better than the "investment" in Credit Suisse and Barclays Bank by Gulf investors during the 2008 financial crisis.

In 2008, like many banks, Credit Suisse and Barclays were technically bankrupt by the financial crisis: their liabilities exceeded their reserves. In the crisis, insolvent banks had three options:

1. Get an explicit government bail-out (take government money, which is what many banks did);

2. Raise capital from private investors (which is what a few, mainly better capitalised banks did); or

3. Receive an implicit bail-out (the government offers some guarantees, the central bank buys your not-so-good assets for cash at an above-market price, etc. This is what the rest received).

Credit Suisse and Barclays came up with a better plan: they created their own money and "loaned" it to "investors" from the Gulf. As with normal credit money creation, on the banks' books there was an asset (a loan) and a deposit (of the loan amount, for the use of the investors; this is FV money). The investors then used this newly created FV money to purchase newly issued preference shares in the banks. So, on the liabilities side of the balance sheet, the banks no longer had a deposit obligation; instead, they had brand *new capital in the bank!* What collateral did the Gulf investors put up as security for the "loan"? Well, they put up their newly received preference shares. Can you see the *illusion?*

Try not to laugh, but there is an entire regulatory regime for calculating "capital adequacy ratios" for banks. [45] The same banks that can create their own money and their own capital. To make sure that the banks have sufficient "tiers" of capital for the risk they undertake. So, don't worry, the regulators have it all under control.

Wait a minute, you may be asking: even if these Gulf investors didn't put up a penny of the billions of new "capital" that was created, they still have to pay the interest on the billions in loan "money" they received, right? The answer is no. Don't worry for the Gulf investors. Barclays made a transfer to the investors of £322 million as part of the "investment". You read that right: the only physical cash transfer in relation to the investment of £3 billion in Barclays went from Barclays to the Gulf investors. What was the £322 million for? Well, Barclays doesn't need to reveal that. For Credit Suisse, there were convertible elements to the loan too complex for you to understand, gentle reader. [46]

The bail-out of UBS during the financial crisis used up almost all the funds available to the Federal treasury in Switzerland, at a significant cost to every single Swiss taxpayer. When it came to Credit Suisse's deception, the regulator allowed it to pass. If Swiss citizens knew how their two global banks actually functioned and the risk that is borne by the Swiss people, they would never support these banks.

In the United Kingdom something strange happened: the Serious Fraud Office called it a fraud. The SFO is a minor regulator and doesn't usually get involved in such matters. The main British bank regulator is the prestigious Financial Conduct Authority, which did nothing. Undoubtedly, it found Barclays' conduct to be just fine. Eventually, the British establishment courts examined the "loan", found nothing that could indicate any fraud whatsoever, and dismissed the SFO's case. The traditional British sense of fair play prevailed.

Why did this "loan" for capital injection work? Because of confidence. Because people believed in this self-created "money". To make it believable, you need believable investors, of course. When you want to arrange something like this, you are better off calling people from the Gulf rather than from, say,

---

45 Capital adequacy standards are overseen by the Bank for International Settlements in Basel, Switzerland.

46 The heart of the loan - investment in bank capital are summarised here. Of course, if you do something so plain vanilla, it is obvious to many, even those who are not financial specialists. So, naturally, the overall dealings between these two banks and the Gulf investors was made much more complex, involving: offshore companies; other, complex financing instruments; detailed legal documents, etc. The core issue is that the banks created their own money to facilitate believable "investors" to purchase shares, so that the banks' capital adequacy ratios could be reported at higher, adequate levels but with no true change in value.

Mauritania. Actually, in some ways, you could say that the Gulf investors provided an extremely valuable service. Just not in cash. They provided confidence capital. For Barclays and Credit Suisse, rational actors in the economy, this confidence capital was obviously more valuable than a government bail-out.

Think that this process doesn't happen in your country? Well, I'm sure it doesn't.

Whether you want to call it a con game, an illusion, or a fraud, it is on confidence that the fractional reserve banking system exists and nothing else. It makes people dishonest, in a way, because Barclays and Credit Suisse cannot just come out and tell the truth about why it was really done: to encourage depositors to believe that the banks were solid, that their money is there and safe, to prevent a bank run. It is the intrinsic, dishonest nature of "fractional" reserve banking. Your money cannot be "there" and also lent out. No bank is "solid". If you lose the confidence of depositors and they withdraw their funds above a certain amount, any fractional reserve bank would just collapse.

**Takeaways**

1. Banks create their own money. Academic studies prove it. Some central banks (partially) admit it. If you worked deeply in a bank, you know it.
2. Bank can also create their own capital.
3. Trying to regulate banks by evaluating their capital adequacy ratios is a joke.
4. This money creation ability is in the hands of the 1%.

# 4
# HOW ARE THE 1% CONNECTED, GLOBALLY?

Think that the 1% are not connected? Think that they are just individuals, not a group? Well, of course they have their own unique characters and businesses, but they are also linked, economically. Even if they don't always agree or like each other, they all have similar, inter-connected financial incentives that give them a common position on issues that matter to them. They are not a monolithic block, coordinating actions through some central organisation, of course. But, their inter-connections have significant influence on society and is best seen during financial crises.

This chapter will lay the foundations for understanding the 1%'s commonality of purpose. For this, we need to start with learning how money moves from bank to bank.

### Where do the connections start?

What if the borrower transfers his deposit to another bank? Why would Bank B accept Bank A's newly created credit money?

Now we are really starting to get somewhere in solving the mystery.

To return to our example: our borrower gets $10,625 in a deposit account that the bank creates for them. Remember that deposit accounts are liabilities for a bank; it is something that the bank owes to the borrower. Now suppose that the borrower uses these funds to pay a supplier, for a piece of equipment, and the money is transferred to the supplier's bank, Bank B. As the customer, you just transferred "money" but what happens between these two banks?

Now, Bank B would have an IOU to the supplier, which they will have to pay out of their future earnings. But, how does this balance, as they don't have an asset?

(i.e. they didn't make a loan to the supplier, so they don't expect a future income stream from them). It isn't PV money (meaning, it isn't money representing value already created, with no loan attached to it). It is FV money, but the future cashflows are going to Bank A, not to Bank B! Do you think that Bank B is going to accept a liability without a corresponding asset? [47] So, how is this solved? This is part of the mystery. When you solve it, you will be one of the few people in the world who really understands money and banking.

Well, to keep it simple, let's assume that the two banks have a direct relationship with each other, which means that each bank has an account at the other bank. [48] This allows Bank A to "transfer" $10,625 to the supplier's bank, Bank B. There are two main aspects to the transfer: a message system (like SWIFT), for notifications, and reciprocal bank accounts, where money is exchanged between banks. Bank A would credit $10,625 into the account that Bank B holds at Bank A. This is how banks settle transfers. In most cases, it is a long, complex process that takes at least several days to reconcile. It is also a transfer of risk from Bank A to Bank B. Bank B takes on an obligation to pay the supplier, in return for "money" from Bank A. The supplier's bank is receiving FV credit money from Bank A, so they now have exposure to Bank A's credit risk (like, do they make good lending decisions?), their future performance. [49] When you multiply that by millions of transfers each day in the banking system, you begin to understand why almost all fractional reserve banks are inter-linked globally via credit money creation. You begin to understand how *credit crises* are transmitted around the world.

You might argue that you can create credit money just between two entities, without needing a bank. This is somewhat true. If a purchaser gives a supplier a year to pay, the supplier has additional purchasing power, with no bank

---

47 This is another reason why it doesn't make sense to say that banks create credit money out of "nothing". When you get into the technical details, what happens when the deposit that corresponds to credit money is transferred to another bank? The other bank likely wants to have something to back the new deposit liability they are taking on. Probably they won't accept it if you say you created it out of "nothing", so you will give them a little bit of that "nothing" as security.

48 This is a simplification, but the main point is the same regardless of the intermediary system. It is also possible that the banks don't have a direct relationship, so they use a middleman, a correspondent bank. They could also use some intermediary system or they could both have accounts at the central bank that could be used for offsets. Most involve pure FV money, but some have a mix of PV and FV money.

49 Again, this is a simplification. Many transfers between banks are netted out and calculated at some future period, either intra-day or at the end of the day or later. In some circumstances, settlement is via holdings at a central bank. However, the main point is the same: commercial banks create the vast amount of "money" in our economy, through the deposit (IOU) process. These IOUs are backed by only about 10% of your deposited cash. Most of the repayment obligation is linked to expected FV profits. This credit money, in deposit accounts, is accepted by other banks as "money", which creates the link between banks.

involved. However, this isn't really money creation. This grant of a year to pay isn't very liquid. It is unlikely you can buy a cup of coffee with it. To be accepted as "money" you need an entire system. Other entities (like other banks) need to accept credit between entities as money. [50]

Acceptance of other banks' credit money (either as bank issued paper or in the form of deposit accounts) was always one of the key issues in the formation of central banks and, in particular, in the debate over their role as lender of last resort. [51] In fact, in the United States, many smaller banks, particularly the ones that dealt with "the little guy" type of borrowers (farmers, blue collar labourers, small businesses in the Western states), were originally excluded from the Federal Reserve System.

**How bank money grows over time.**

A single bank can create credit money on its own. As this money moves through the financial system, deposits into other banks have two important effects:

1. The deposit money into other banks leads to further lending and money creation, after these banks set a certain amount aside (the "fractional reserve").

2. The inter-links between banks are mainly credit risk. [52]

---

50 An example is Switzerland. The Swiss, being a free people, do not allow their government to restrict their right to create money. There is a second currency in Switzerland, called the WIR, that is used mainly amongst small and medium size enterprises and has been in place for almost 100 years. Perhaps that is why bitcoin is also accepted for many transactions, like on Swiss trains, to pay taxes in some places, etc. In contrast, in the United States, citizens have wide freedoms but have no right to create their own money, even amongst consenting adults, so to speak. You can say what you want, bear arms, vote, etc., but if you try to create your own money, armed government agents will show up pretty quickly to stop you. Now you have touched a nerve. Now you see what is really important to the 1%

51 The economics profession is second only to the funeral business in using euphemisms. Lender of last resort actually means that you have driven your bank into the ground and it is about to go bankrupt. No one will deal to you, because they suspect your loans (needed to support the FV credit money you have created) are not very good. The government can lend to you because it can just print more money into existence. That means that the rest of us are all worse off, because inflation takes value (purchasing power) away from us. But, just a little bit for each of us, so most of us don't notice the theft. Normal businesses, like the ones run by the 99%, can fail if things go wrong. Ordinary people can lose their jobs if things go wrong. The 1% has a "lender of last resort".

52 A small element of value exchanged between banks is PV money, but the majority is FV money, which intrinsically includes credit risk.

Here is how it works.

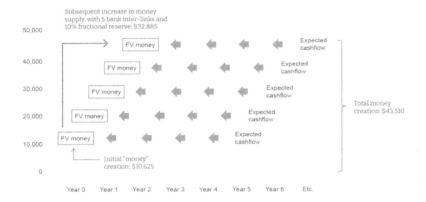

In our example, a borrower started with nothing in their account and then received a loan of $10,625. With a 10% reserve ratio decided on by the banks in the system and after 5 iterations, $43,510 of "money" has been created. All of this money is FV money: the purchasing power created today is dependent on expected future cashflows from the real economy.

**How banks make profit.**

Banks make a profit by lending money at an interest rate that is much higher than their costs of funds. They mainly create their own credit money, which has purchasing power today, in return for the promise of future cashflows from borrowers in the future.

Of course, diversified banks also have other revenue streams. For example, they take your deposit money and use it in "proprietary" activities (you'll appreciate the irony of the name), like sales and trading, market making, wealth management, direct investments, etc.

**How banks don't make profit.**

Banks are not simply intermediaries, charging for connecting surplus capital with productive opportunities. They are not neutral actors in the economy. That is the Walt Disney version of helpful, friendly banks and it is almost completely a lie.

Here is an illustration of how banks really operate.

### The Wizard of JP Morgan

"OMG! You don't just function as an intermediary, helpfully matching excess savings with productive uses, like what I read in those economics textbooks. You are actually creating your own money!"

### Takeaways

1. Banks create their own money. In addition, through the deposit process amongst banks, globally, the fractional reserve banking system itself also creates money.
2. Banks, central banks, dishonest economists and other enablers state that banks don't create money themselves. This is a complete lie.
3. These players are part of, and inextricably intertwined with, the 1%. They also state that banks are relatively neutral actors in an economy, just channeling depositors' savings to loans. This is also a complete lie.
4. The 1% are connected, globally, through the banking system.

# 5
# HOW CAN YOU CALCULATE THE WEALTH OF THE 1%?

Well, you have to start with banks. Bored out of your mind yet? Yeah, that is the reason that the power of the 1% is so poorly understood.

Why should we concentrate on banks? It is like the bank robber Willie Sutton replied, when they asked him why he was so obsessed with banks. He said: "Because that's where the money is." "Duh", Homer Simpson probably would have replied. If you want to understand the 1%, understand power in society, understand inequality, understand money and the economy, you had better get as interested in banks as Willie Sutton was.

**How to value banks.**

Here is an illustration from one of the industry standard books on valuation. [53]

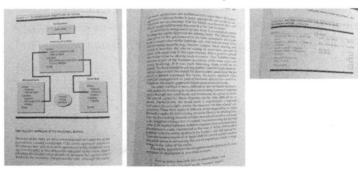

53 T. Copeland et al., *Valuation: Measuring and Managing the Value of Companies*, 2nd edn., Hoboken, John Wiley & Sons, 1994, pp. 498 - 499, 503.

So, the textbooks tell you <u>not</u> to value a bank like a normal firm that makes profit-seeking investments based on risk and return. How should you value a bank? You should imagine the bank as separate profit units and then value each of them separately since, unlike normal firms, they create value on the liabilities side of the balance sheet. In your imagination, you should artificially assume that each unit has its own imaginary cost of capital that it charges internally to other units. In their example for "ABC Bank", the "Wholesale bank" makes a spread of 12 - 8% (the 8% is completely fictitious) borrowing from the "Treasury and trading" unit (the numbers for which, conveniently, are never, ever revealed by banks) and the "Retail bank" takes in deposits from the public and their profit, from lending to the internal Treasury, is 8 - 5% (which is also completely fictitious). Just banks as financial intermediaries with a little bit of treasury management. Sure, maybe this is how ABC Bank works. Maybe ABC Bank is also where the Tooth Fairy does her banking.

Here is some text from a typical business school class on valuing financial services companies. [54]

*Unlike manufacturing firms that invest in plant, equipment and other fixed assets, financial service firms invest primarily in intangible assets such as brand name and human capital. Consequently, their investments for future growth often are categorized as operating expenses in accounting statements. Not surprisingly, the statement of cash flows to a bank show little or no capital expenditures and correspondingly low depreciation.*

*With working capital, we run into a different problem. If we define working capital as the difference between current assets and current liabilities, a large proportion of a bank's balance sheet would fall into one or the other of these categories. Changes in this number can be both large and volatile and may have no relationship to reinvestment for future growth.*

*As a result of this difficulty in measuring reinvestment, we run into two practical problems in valuing these firms.*

*The first is that we cannot estimate cash flows without estimating reinvestment. In other words, if we cannot identify how much a bank is reinvesting for future growth, we cannot identify cash flows either.*

54 Class handout, London Business School, MSc degree in Finance programme, from a visiting professor from a US business school

*The second is that estimating expected future growth becomes more difficult if the reinvestment rate cannot be measured.*

Yeah. Raise your hand if you can spot the *circularity* here.

Other than these little problems, valuing banks is easy.

Economists, consultants, "industry experts", etc. mostly have three things in common when it comes to banks:

1. They have never worked in core banking, never made a loan, never written code for loan algorithms, never seen the internal, management loan accounting.

2. They never mention in their work that banks create money (credit money, FV money) through the loan process.

3. They break out in a cold sweat when confronted with the reality of bank processes, as it is so counter to the view of how banks operate that they learned about themselves when they were students.

Banks are *intentionally opaque*. Intentionally hard for outsiders to understand. There is a reason you are made to feel stupid or uncomfortable when your mind wanders to thinking about how banks work, or to define what money really is. It is the same reason that the precious metal depositories and guilds from the Middle Ages were impenetrable. What could that reason be?

What a mystery.

### What happens if someone cannot repay a loan?

When a borrower cannot repay a loan, it means that the asset that the bank has created (the loan) is worth less than expected; potentially, it is worth zero. That is a problem, because the bank has already created money and put it in a deposit account for the borrower. This is FV money; it is dependent on the future cashflows from the loan. If there are no future cashflows coming in from the borrower then this created money, theoretically, has no value.

However, it is a bit tricky. Your borrower has already taken this money and paid their supplier, which is annoying. So, the worthless FV money is now in the supplier's bank (technically, you, the bank, put FV money into an account for the supplier's bank, to make it all balance in the system). So, now that money isn't any good; it doesn't just disappear, like the loan. Worse, the deposit leads the other bank to think they have more "money". So, they create more loans (and more money), on the basis of this deposit of "money" that they have received.

Loan failures cause the *recursive destruction* of credit money in the same way that credit money creation leads to more credit money creation. When borrowers cannot repay loans, it destroys an asset to the bank. The asset is mainly matched to FV credit money that was created. This FV money is now also worthless and the bank has to find other assets to support the FV money that they created. These other assets can be from reserves, deposits of PV money, and/or borrowings. This causes banks to reduce their lending, as their assets have been reduced, resulting in an impact on the real economy. When this process happens at scale, when it is inter-linked amongst banks and the recursive destruction of credit money is significant for the fractional reserve banking industry, it causes an excessive downward variance in the business cycle.

How it works is set out below.

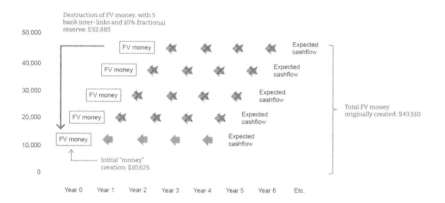

Let's imagine that your initial loan is expected to be ok. So, you expect to get in $14,875 over the next five years, of which you created FV money today of $10,675 and gave it to the borrower. However, the other 4 loans that were made all go bust. That is a problem, as they are linked to a further

$32,885 of FV money that was created in the system as a result of your initial loan. (Actually, based on typical multipliers, much more money would be created, but let's be conservative for our illustration). So, $10,675 +

$32,885 = $43,510 of FV money has been created, but the expected cashflow to be received in the future is only $14,875, which comes in over the next 5 years. If you are not a math wizz, just know that these numbers are bad for the economy.

Now you understand the 2008 financial crisis a bit better.

**How do banks value themselves?**

Well, they don't tell you. They don't really want you to know. Of all of the industries covered by research analysts in investment banks, financial services firms are the most difficult to evaluate and then forecast. Banks just don't make the necessary details available. None of them do. It is a "trade secret".

You now know most of the important aspects of how banks operate. It isn't so important to know many of the remaining details. You are not going to go set up a fractional reserve banking operation, I hope.

The main thing to understand about banks is that while most of their assets (loans) have a finite life, like, say 5 years, the bank itself is correctly conceived of internally as a perpetuity. It is basically an on-going bundle of expected future loans, converting future cashflow streams into purchasing power today. This is its monetisation role.

So, you can think of valuing a bank, or a business unit of a bank, using a perpetuity growth formula, as set out below. [55]

$$= \frac{CF}{r - g}$$

Where,

**CF** is the expected cashflow in the period (either t0 or at the start of some Terminal Value period)
**r** is a discount rate, the cost of capital
**g** is the expected future growth rate

If the perpetuity is for a future period, then the derived value needs to be discounted back to a present value.

Banks have a perception of their own value and adjust their actions accordingly. People are the same. If you feel good about future economic prospects, feel secure, feel positive about the potential for continued employment, a raise or a bonus, you are more likely to loosen the purse strings and spend now. If you feel insecure about the future, you are likely to conserve your funds.

---

55 This is a simplification and you can add many different valuation considerations. The main point here is: keep your eyes focused on "g".

For the bank, what drives their actions is "g" in the formula. That is their perception of the future. The term "g" has significantly greater influence on bank lending volumes than the term "r". This is one of the reasons why typical central bank policy action is so ineffective when it comes to aggregate lending in an economy. The correlation between r and aggregate lending is low. The correlation between banks' perception of g and aggregate lending is high.

## How the banking system works, globally.

Credit money creation by commercial banks and the fact that most commercial banks accept deposit account transfers from other banks lead to the inter-linking of credit risk.

Here are some lessons from this global inter-linking of credit.

- One, small bank undertaking fractional reserve banking is high risk. Banks know that bigger is better and that scale is important to mitigate the risks inherent in this banking model. If you are a bank, you want to be too big to fail.

- Or, you want to be as connected as possible to other banks, like through correspondent banking. Everyone needs to be in on it. Globally. Success in fractional reserve banking requires coordination and enablers. Over the centuries, a vast infrastructure has grown up to enforce the system (legal, police, debt collection, prisons, etc.). It is the same in almost every country, regardless of political leanings.

## Takeaways

1. No bank reveals key information to outsiders to allow them to analyse the bank.
2. The 1% owns most of the banks and is also the best "customers" of these banks.
3. The 1% gets preferential loans from banks.
4. Bank loans are assets for the bank. They make loans mainly as principals, not agents, and are driven by their own, principal profit- motives.
5. Almost all banks are functionally inter-connected globally. The global 1% are all incentivised to support the banking industry.

# 6
# GLOBAL FINANCIAL CRISES ... AND THE SAFTEY NET FOR THE 1%

When a crisis hits the economy, most of the 1% are in a different position than the rest of us. Here is why. First, like usual, a little more on the banking system, this time from a global perspective.

**How financial crises are caused.**

The vast majority of financial crises are caused when there is a recursive destruction of bank credit money that was used for the third lending area: against asset prices.

Recall that lending to the first two areas (productive investments, like extending the plant or hiring more workers; and time shifting of consumption) are both based on expected future cashflows. Maybe those cashflows will materialise, maybe they will be a little higher or lower. In extreme cases, maybe they will be zero.

Financing assets is different, though. It assumes that an asset will increase in value in the future, which is how the loan gets paid off. Maybe you sell the stock to someone else at a higher price, or you hold the real estate expecting prices to rise and then you will sell it to someone else.

If future, higher prices for that asset do not materialise, however, there are two problems for the bank, on each side of the balance sheet. On the asset side, well, your asset has gone down. The stock or real estate tied to your loan is worth less. That is a problem because your loan is only backed by the asset value; there is no (or little) cashflows that can be used to repay the loan. Your other problem is on the liabilities side. You created credit money and gave it to the borrower, which is now gone. This is FV money; it is tied to the expected future value of the loan, your asset (which is now underwater). It isn't PV money (which has no link to future cashflows, since it represents value already created); it is FV money, which is a lot more dangerous.

If, as is typical, the borrower used this credit money to pay their own suppliers, then this will have involved transferring money from the account at your bank to accounts at other banks. As we saw with how transfers work, this means that the suppliers received a deposit from their bank. The way that this works in the banking system, you will have credited the other bank's account. So, you owe money to the other bank, which allowed this other bank to put money in the deposit account of the person receiving the money, the supplier.

But, now, the asset (the loan) you were counting on to bring in money isn't there. Sadly, however, the money you credited into this other bank's account is still there. You still owe them the money. You wish you didn't make the loan in the first place: the value of the asset in the market is uncertain and it doesn't produce cashflow. At the same time, the other bank, the bank of the supplier, has excitedly received a new deposit, put some aside in reserve, and happily lent out 90% of what they received. You want to call them and say, hey, maybe best to just hold on to that "money" until we can figure out the value of the asset, linked to the original loan. Now, this decline in asset prices has caused a problem for you. It has also transmitted some of that problem to the supplier's bank, which they don't really know about. It doesn't stop there, though, as the supplier's bank has also lent out some of this money, so some other bank also now has a credit problem. Isn't fractional reserve banking a great system?

The graph below illustrates the effect of increasing asset valuations over the economic cycle. In this case, they increase from 100 to 305, which is a 25% uplift per transaction for the asset.

The bank finances the asset at a prudent 80% loan to value ratio. The key issue is: what is the value level? Suppose the value is set by the market (like for stocks or real estate) and you mechanically apply your 80% LTV ratio, as is standard in banks. The problem occurs when value resets in the market and the price falls.

The problem with bank lending against assets is illustrated below.

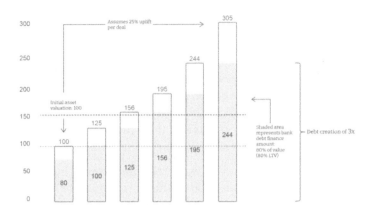

The result of a decline in value of the asset should be obvious:

- The bank debt doesn't also automatically reset; the bank has already made the loan, based on the (now too high) valuation. All of a sudden, LTV is way too high.

- In creating the loan, the bank created a deposit and FV credit money. This is what was lent to the borrower. It also doesn't reset. This is also based on a valuation that was too high. So, too high LTV = creation of high risk FV credit money in the economy.

- There are no (or little) cashflows to support the loan (and the FV credit money created).

- This leads to FV credit money destruction.

- Banks' inter-linked accounts transmit this value destruction in a recursive manner throughout the economy.

Oh, but wait: the textbooks tell me that banks don't create money! And, that I should not value banks as if there are making investments, like normal firms! Here is the truth: banks create the vast majority of "money" in the economy and they make investments (called loans, the assets on their balance sheet) with the objective of making a profit. Don't be deceived.

This combination (FV credit money creation + use of this money to finance asset purchases + inter-links amongst banks) is what caused the 1929 Great Depression (stock value declines) and the 2008 Great Recession (housing value declines). Essentially, long-run natural valuation levels became distorted (too elevated) by credit money creation, which caused a concomitant series of further distortions to natural asset valuation levels. Natural asset valuation levels are those valuation levels that would be set by supply and demand for an asset (based on risk and return metrics) in the absence of bank credit money.

Here is a graph of what the Federal Reserve in the United States terms the "Adjusted Monetary Base". [56]

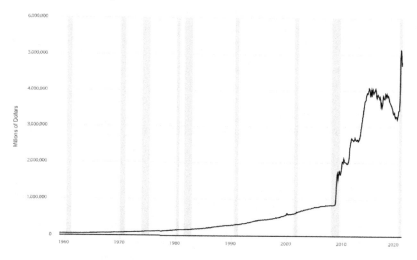

Shaded areas indicate recessions.

Here is the key take-away from the graph:

*Under a fractional reserve banking system, recessions are a regular occurrence. Recessions are <u>an inherent part</u> of fractional reserve banking. Recessions are the norm, not the exception. No one should be surprised when the economy experiences excess variance, which is mainly caused by bank credit money creation used for asset purchase finance.*

(Another take-away might be, given the astronomical amount of "money" created by central banks over the past decade, that the next bust in the economy might be on a scale we have never before experienced).

---

56 Federal Reserve Bank of St. Louis. Data from 1 January 1918 to 1 August 2020. Where are the data series on credit money creation by banks? What about details of credit money used to finance asset purchases? No such data. You can get data on how many vacuum cleaners were sold in each state, but nothing on the statics that really matter for evaluating excess economic variance.

You can see from the graph that it doesn't matter if you are on the gold standard or not; *it is the fractional reserve banking system itself that creates recessions.* It is not the gold that is the determining factor. It is the IOU.

When bank credit money is used to finance assets that subsequently decline in value, banks have effectively created purchasing power for which there are no future cashflows. The value that a bank ascribed to an asset, like real estate or stocks, is never going to be there; the value doesn't exist. And, there is no cashflow coming from the asset to pay back the loan ... which the created "money" was based on. Value impairment through the recursive destruction of credit money linked to asset financing is what causes most of the downward excess variance in the business cycle.

There is a reason why the love of money is the root of all evil. The 1%'s banking system distorts our memory of value created, as well as our values. It causes us to be less human.

**How do banks protect themselves against recessions?**

Modern, fractional reserve banking is an *inherently risky* activity.

Here is why:

1.  The core philosophy of fractional reserve banking is *based on dishonesty.* The bank tells depositors that it is their money, sitting in their account, and they can have it back at any time. At the same time, the bank lends most of the money to borrowers or uses it themselves, including as an input to their own credit money creation. The fundamental premise of fractional reserve banking is built on a lie. [57] This lie is then propagated by the 1%, the banks' enablers in society and enforced by the state.

2.  These banks create their own "money" today, which has current purchasing power and which they give to borrowers. The value of this money, however, is dependent on future cashflows. If these future cashflows do not materialise, *recursive credit money destruction causes economic crises* and means that the bank may not have enough reserves to cover the lie that they told depositors: that they could have their money back.

---

[57] Here is an interesting moral question: can you be both a decent human being who believes in telling the truth and, at the same time, even in your own small way, be a supporter of the fractional reserve banking system?

The structure of a typical bank is illustrated below.

Even a small change in "g", the growth number used in the valuation formula for future cashflows, has a significant impact on the calculation of banks' asset values. That is the reason why most banks don't lend much again during/after a recession, regardless of the price of money set by the central bank. The money price (part of their cost of funds) is a component of asset value, but is much less important than the "g" estimate.

**The risk structure of fractional reserve banking:**
**An inverted house of cards**

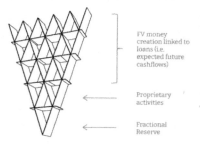

The *value of "g"* causes a wide variance in the estimated future value of a bank's assets, the cards at the top of the inverted pyramid. As the amount held in reserve is small compared to the expected future value of the assets forecasted into the future, the effect is that systemic shocks in the economy can wipe out the PV money valuation of many banks. In the old days, there would (rightly) be a bank run. In 2008, after the collapse of Lehman Brothers, many large, global banks quietly admitted to their home governments that their reserves were insufficient to cover the FV money liabilities that they had created or acquired from others, that they were insolvent. Hence, the bail-out of the 1% banks by society, cleverly disguised by most governments through the use of euphemistic language to describe what they are doing. Not sure what quantitative easing is? Well, it is injecting newly printed money into the economy banking system, which disproportionately benefits the 1%. Has that prompted the helpful banks- as-simple-financial-intermediaries to lend again? No. What will cause them to lend again? Well, it will be their internal, profit-motive-driven estimate of the value of "g". Their estimate of future expected cashflows to their assets (loans).

So, as a bank, how do you protect yourself against the risk of failure? The answers are set out below.

1.  Bank contributions pay the salaries of the regulators, in most countries.

2.  Scale is important: banks want to be as big and diversified as possible to handle shocks. Then, you can get yourself labelled "systemically important" or "too big to fail" by your enablers at the regulatory

agencies.

3. Banks contribute to politicians, who set the rules governing the banks.

4. Banks, and their enablers, attack any other financial system that poses a threat to the fractional reserve system.

Some commercial bank insiders, perhaps more cynical or more versed in game theory, have a different approach to protecting against future recessions: *do nothing*. Recessions are a given. In good times, when a bank makes profits, it (and the bankers) receive the benefits. In a mild recession, banks suffer losses, but they are not enough to threaten to topple the inverted house of cards. In a bad recession, everyone panics. Globally. Regardless of the political party in office. In these recessions, all commercial banks are saved by the government. The establishment unites around euphemistically labelled bank rescues, since the establishment needs, and benefits from, the banking system. That means that the government, whether it is obvious or not, takes a little bit from everyone in society to replenish the PV money at the bottom of the inverted house of cards.

From a purely game theoretic approach in regard to payoffs, it is certainly the banks' dominant strategy to do nothing, while still performing all of the relatively low-cost public relations exercises.

**Takeaways**

1. Our current banking system sucks.
2. Bank money creation used for asset purchase financing causes most of the booms and busts in the business cycle.
3. Like death and taxes, recessions are something to be expected, not surprised by.
4. Banks really are better viewed, technically, as a bundle of real options based on the expected future value of loan cashflows and the current value of the money they have created.
5. Banks, money creation, and the 1% are so intertwined that it is hard to separate them.

# 7
# WHO ENABLES THE 1%?

Some of the 1% get there because they are incredibly intelligent, hard-working, and create a lot of value for society, like Elon Musk. Many others get there because they have preferential access to bank money, on the best terms. But, who enables this money system for the 1%? Isn't it regulated? Let's find out.

**Regulation.**

We now know that the power to create the money supply in an economy is granted to banks. We know as well that bank credit money is tied to loans, which are just expected future cashflow streams. Essentially, a bank gives its borrower customer "money" today in return for the promise by the borrower of paying more money in the future. In its decision-making about loans (and money creation), a bank undertakes its operations driven by a profit motive.

This grant of money creation powers to banks raises some ethical issues, some of which are set out below.

1.  Society grants the exclusive right to commercial banks to create credit money in an economy. [58]

2.  Banks create this credit money with the objective of maximizing<profits to their shareholders.

3.  This credit money is freely insured by the government, which provides a massive subsidiary to the banking sector. [59]

---

[58] This is FV money (dependent on future economic outcomes). PV money (which is not tied to any repayment) can only be created by the government.

[59] There is an explicit maximum amount per deposit account that is insured. Implicitly, all monies in a banking system are insured. For many governments, on an economic benefit basis, this is their

4.  Bank regulation is determined by the political sector, including granting money creation rights, subsidies and restriction on use of funds for loans.

5.  Banks make significant transfers to the political sector.

6.  If banks make a profit, these profits are retained by the shareholders of the bank.

7.  If banks fail, the cost of failure, including recapitalisation, are borne mainly by society.

Since the deposits of a bank are insured by the government, it is a significant advantage to the banks. In addition to banks being granted the right to create credit money, which forms the vast majority of money in the economy <u>and</u> is used exclusively to the advantage of their private shareholders (with significant representation by the 1%), the government <u>also</u> provides an *enormous subsidy* to these banks in the form of *free deposit insurance*.[60] Free deposit insurance does not only artificially increase bank profits, it also creates an extremely serious moral hazard issue, which contributes to the excess variance in the business cycle. Imagine for a moment that the banks themselves had to pay their own insurance premiums, either to the government or to a private sector insurance company. If ordinary businesses had free insurance on everything that they did, do you think that might impact their behaviour?

largest single transfer of value after Defence, Social Security, Education, and Healthcare. Governments can usually satisfy this bank insurance obligation in a way that is seemingly costless (or even beneficial) to government, by printing money and causing inflation. Inflation reduces the liabilities of the government (hence, it is a benefit to the government). However, satisfying this insurance by printing money has a cost to society: it leads to those who have savings being worse off, as it essentially takes purchasing power from them.

60 Insurance is the best descriptive term to use to give confidence to "depositors", but it is not really insurance. When you insure your house in case of fire, the insurance company has a fund available to cover claims. With government "deposit" insurance, there is no such pot of money. If the government needs to bail out the financial sector (that is right: like what has happened for the past 10 years and what continues today), they print the money. They don't take it from an insurance fund. In some cases, for window dressing, banks make transfers to the government for the costs of the regulator/insurance/guarantee agency, but these are not insurance premiums, calculated as premiums would be if there were an insurance fund. They call it different names so nobody freaks out and takes up arms, but it is newly created money. Who pays for all of this "insurance" that props up the banking sector? You do: the tax payer. Hard to believe that it isn't really insurance? Don't worry, it isn't really a deposit, either. The correct way to understand the guarantees behind fractional reserve banking is that the ~~deposit~~ loan from you to the bank is backed by a ~~government insurance policy~~ promise to print more money so that the bank can ~~give you back your deposit~~ pay back the loan from you, (just with less value, meaning less purchasing power, caused by the newly created money process; a little tax from the 99% to help ~~the 1%~~ the banks).

**Reform?**

- If you are getting all excited about ...
- the possibilities to restrict banks from lending their credit money to finance asset purchases as a way to reduce excess variance in the business cycle, or
- getting banks to pay the costs of deposit insurance to reduce moral hazard, or
- banning banks from making political contributions, or
- putting warning labels on deposit accounts that tell people the truth about them really lending their savings to the bank and that the bank can do whatever it wants with the money, which is no longer theirs ...
- etc.

... you need to keep in mind that large parts of the establishment is enmeshed as enablers of this fractional reserve banking system. Millions of people's livelihoods depend on society not seeing behind the curtain, to see what banks really do. It will be a *David versus a Goliath-on-steroids* fight and, even if you succeeded with this reform, fractional reserve banking is still inherently dishonest and flawed.

There is a new, better system that is emerging as an alternative. One that doesn't rely on the banks. Technically, it is a digital system, compared to the analog system that is traditional banking. It is an alternative that doesn't have all of the moral perversity of the old fractional reserve system. One that restores the concept of memory of value created through productive effort in the economy. One that aligns with our most basic human values. There is a new technology alternative that is like sunlight, a needed disinfectant to the sick system in which we now live. We will get to it later, but first you need to understand who really enables the 1% and their banking system.

**Central banks.**

What is the main role of central bankers in regulating the current economic system?

If you have seen the graph above of economic booms and busts occurring like clockwork over the past century, you might be tempted to burst out laughing at this question. You might conclude, on the evidence, that central bankers are ineffective. However, you might be being too kind to them, so let's look at the details.

Let's imagine that being a central banker was a real job, like being an engineer

47

or a software developer or a medical doctor. The main objectives for a central banker are *price stability* and *employment*. Well, here is a chart of the purchasing power of the US dollar since the inception of the Federal Reserve to the end of 2017.

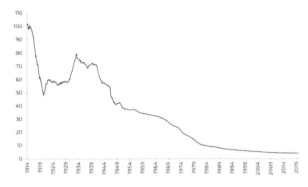

Explains why you don't see too many „Five & Dime" stores in the US anymore. Great work, Fed. It looks like Zimbabwe, just over a longer timeframe.

OK, so the product has lost 95% of its value and you wanted it to be stable. That isn't so great on the CV. But, it has outperformed almost every other nation state currency and that is why it is the global reserve currency today. So, maybe you could argue in your defence, if you were a US central banker, that your performance has sucked, but it has sucked a little less than most of the others. Same with your product: it obviously sucks, too, but a little less than most of the others. [61] Then you remember another form of money: gold. Which somehow has held its value since Neolithic times, even without the benefit of an economics degree, which is *really* irritating. So, in conclusion, central bankers can go home at the end of the day and feel pretty good about their <u>relative</u> performance. Except against that rock.

Let's turn to booms and busts. You recall the chart above. Well, there have been 18 officially recorded recessions over the past 100 years in the United States, of varying length. Let's assume that there were no booms and that recession periods were the only bad periods for price stability. Let's be generous and say that about once in every 10 years there is a system failure. So, what if the same thing happened in engineering? What if we built dams and every 10 years or so they burst? You think people might complain? What if you built smart phones and one in every 10 times you turned it on, it broke? You think people would keep buying your product? What if one in every 10 patients died on your watch? Do you think you would still be practising?

---

61 As hard as it is to believe, there are actually several "stablecoins" tied to the value of the US dollar, with more constantly appearing.

So, why do we accept such failure from central bankers? Why do we just live with such excess variance in the business cycle, its destructive effects on wealth and employment, and its repetition over time?

Where are all of the scholarly research papers on the effects of banks' creating credit money? Where is the analysis of the impact of this credit money and its use for asset purchases? Where are the statistics on the recursive, backward destruction of this credit money when the (mainly arbitrary) asset valuations (which underpinned the credit money creation in the first place) decline below a trigger level, which causes the avalanche effect of credit money destruction? Where are the details on how the global inter-links of banks accepting other banks' FV money transmits financial crises? Well, there is nothing from the economics establishment.

**Central banks and trust.**

Some have argued that it is central banks who engender trust in the banking system. The people who most often make this argument are central bankers. Let's analyse their claim in respect of trust.

The establishment of the Federal Reserve System in the United States provides a good experiment to test whether the presence of a central bank had an impact on the stability of the commercial banking sector. The US central bank was established at the end of 1913. In a comparison of the two decades before and after this date (adjusting for the effects of the Great Depression), there was no significant change in the rate of bank failures. However, from 1933 onwards there were relatively few bank failures. It was the first time in US history that bank failures came relatively to an almost complete halt. What caused this? In 1933, the US created deposit insurance, in an entity separate from the central bank. Now, everyone's bank deposits were insured by the government (at least that was the headline message, without getting into the details). Bank stability has little to do with central bankers or the central bank money rate. It has to do with *insurance* and *confidence* in a bank. Not confidence in central bankers' ability to make wise economic decisions.

Here is another way to look at trust in central banks' management of a country's money: how does the purchasing power of a currency compare to gold? Even better: if people actually trusted bankers (central bankers or commercial bankers), there should be no market for gold as a store of value. We would have discarded gold the way we stopped using shells. The difference between a nation state currency and gold is that central bankers cannot print gold.

## Is monetary policy really as ineffective as the evidence shows?

Speaking of failure, let's have a look at central bankers' preferred policy tool: monetary policy. People talk about monetary policy in reverent tones, as if some small conclave of government bureaucrats that sets the price of money (in supposedly free market, capitalist economies) has some magic crystal ball. People who have nothing better to do with their time actually track their votes at these useless conclaves. I mean, look at the track record: if these people were doctors, would you let them anywhere near you with a scalpel? Anyway, here is why monetary policy is weakly correlated with bank funding costs. [62]

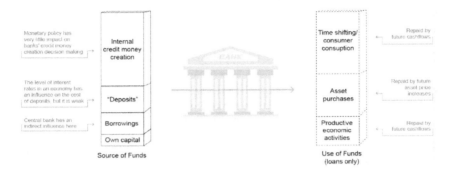

Source of Funds                    Use of Funds
                                   (loans only)

This is an illustration of sources and uses of funds for commercial banks, in regard to loans. Monetary policy is weakly correlated with a commercial bank's actual funding costs; that is why it is so ineffective.

Monetary policy mainly and indirectly affects only one of the four main sources of funds for a bank: borrowing from the central bank. [63] This is a

---

[62] This paper just deals with the main issue: why monetary policy is fundamentally flawed, since it only (indirectly) affects a minority aspect of banks' funding costs. In addition to just being an unsound policy, monetary policy is also ineffective (even if it were not misguided). The policy implementation has a "lag effect" in which it takes months for rate changes to be transmitted through the banking system. Oh, and there are many central banks involved in the process. So, the formula is: committee of government economists + crystal ball looking out at least a year + maybe a half dozen important central banks = policy implementation. Which takes, say, 6 months to filter indirectly through to the economy. You have to be of diminished mental capacity if you think that this is effective. But, don't worry about the efficacy of the policy. The entire approach is a joke. Which we probably should have known, like, 18 recessions ago.

[63] The inter-bank lending market also is impacted by the price of money decisions taken by a central bank, but the effect here is even weaker. The inter-bank market is where banks make loans to each other. The central bank rate is taken into (minor) consideration here but the main determinant is the riskiness of the bank to whom you are lending. So, the inter-bank market prices mainly on credit risk, not what the central bank funds rate is set at. For example, as the 2008 financial crisis unfolded, most central banks lowered their funding rates. Yet, as banks were (rightly) wary of each other's riskiness, rates in the inter-bank market went the opposite way to central bank rates: they went up. Until the market froze, at which time banks were unwilling to lend to each other at any price. This means each

minority of a bank's cost of funds. The largest source of funds is a bank's own internal, credit money creation. The cost of this money is not set by the central bank. As an example, as the good people at Lehman Brothers were packaging up toxic sub-prime mortgages and getting them rated AAA by S&P and Moody's and preparing to sell them to unsuspecting buyers around the world, no one stopped and said, "Wait a minute, what is the Fed Funds rate?" The expected revenue line was so high (and they were not going to hold them on their own books for very long, hopefully) that even if the central bank rate doubled it would have had very little effect on their cost of funds and, consequently, on their expected profits.

Here is a little brain teaser for you:

If commercial banks create the vast majority of money in an economy ... and they do so "out of nothing" (almost, at least in terms of cost of funds), then ... why does the central bank interest rate matter so much? Why do we think that monetary policy is so important? Maybe we cannot see the forest for all of the dots around. Maybe the dot plot is the opiate of the financial masses, that keeps them from seeing fractional reserve banking for what it is.

### The correct punch bowl analogy.

Alan Greenspan remarked that the role of the central bank was to take the punch bowl away just when the party gets going (by which he meant the central bank would raise interest rates when the crystal ball predicts a future upswing in the business cycle; this is using monetary policy to manage the economy). We all know how well that turned out. However, it was his intellectual point that was incorrect, because he doesn't understand how banks actually operate (or isn't telling the truth). It isn't simply an issue of timing. It isn't simply that the Federal Reserve can wait too long to raise interest rates, to pop an asset bubble (or, like 18 of them in the past century).

---

bank was saying to itself: who knows that risks other banks are taking, what FV money creation they have been involved in? This is equivalent to old-fashioned bank runs, where some banks would not take other banks' paper money, because of the credit risk (uh, yeah, how did you create that credit money? Lending to sub-prime borrowers? Lending against stock certificates? Why should I have that risk transferred to me?). In the United States, there was an era in which many banks issued their own money, the so-called Free Banking Era. Most economists will lie to you and tell you that this era is over. In fact, rather than their own bank notes, banks today print their own money in the form of deposit accounts. Which convey purchasing power. Which can be transferred to other banks. Which makes the FV money (tied to a loan) created by the originating bank ... the problem of any linked bank as well. So, banks have two main risk transmission links: the inter-bank lending market and by accepting other bank's deposit money transfers.

The correct point to understand about regulating banks is that:

*They are not drinking your punch, man.*

They have their own punch bowl. And, it is **10x** the size of your punch bowl. And, the mix in their punch is a lot more intoxicating than your punch.

Yeah, of course, they come over and drink out of your punch bowl. And, out of the depositors' punch bowl. But, that is not where the party is.

Alan Greenspan's problem was WYSIATI. What you see is all there is. The cognitive bias described by Daniel Kahneman and Amos Tversky. Perhaps central bankers in their nice offices, and the smug ivory tower economists who surround them, don't spend much time thinking "well, there are still many things I don't know". You see the bankers drinking out of your punch bowl and you assume that is all they have to drink. Well, if banks only got money from the central bank and/or the central bank controlled this money supply through the reserve requirement/money multiplier, then taking the punch bowl away would, indeed, put a damper on the party. But, as explained above, this is a relatively small part of banks' sources of funds, of the money supply, the money supply in the sense of both the gold and the IOU, since both have purchasing power. If you see banks mainly through the lens of the reserve requirement/money multiplier, you would be missing something crucial; you would have fallen into this cognitive bias.

(In addition to the fact that, just by empirical analysis, even taking your own punch bowl away obviously doesn't work, so maybe it is time to revisit your mental model. "Duh", even by common sense observation it *obviously doesn't work*, Homer Simpson would say).

Likewise, if the banks only got money from depositors, if banks were only financial intermediaries, then taking the punch bowl away would be effective. But, again, this is a relatively small part of the money supply. If you see banks mainly through the lens of them as financial intermediaries, you would also be missing something crucial; again, you would have fallen into this cognitive bias.

## So, who is right?

The proof can only be in the empirical results. These results are not in favour of the reserve requirement/money multiplier theory, nor the idea that banks only act as financial intermediaries. Nor do the results support the effectiveness of monetary policy in managing economic variances.

*Raising rates doesn't end the party. [64] Cutting rates doesn't bring the party back to life.*

If you see banks for what they really are, if you really understand money, then you know which punch bowl to take away.

However, even if you do understand the situation, there are a few fatal errors that arise due to the fractional reserve banking system, which are set out below.

1. We are not talking about a physical punch bowl, of course. We are talking about raising central bank interest rates. This mainly just

---

64 Ignore, for the moment, the arrogance that a small group of government functionaries sees the future better than the knowledge that is diffused throughout society, that the centralised few are better than the decentralised community. And, that these supposed visionaries then do the right thing for the economy. You only need to look at the graphs of purchasing power and recessions to have this idea dispelled in your mind. Of course, rate changes do have an impact on financial markets, which are primarily PV money. However, the correlation between rate changes and bank lending volumes, as well as on deposit and borrowing rates, is very low.

influences central bank money, [65] not a bank's FV credit money (which has its own costs and is dependent on future expected cashflows as the main drivers). As central bank money is a relatively minor source of funds for banks, changing the cost of this money will have a weak impact on a bank's behaviour. Consequently, monetary policy is relatively ineffective.

2. Interest rates are a blunt instrument; they cannot be targeted to where the problem is, which is almost always the third use of funds: asset purchases. Interest rates are raised across the economy, affecting also the other two uses of funds: productive investment and time-shifting of consumption. This causes dislocation in the economy and distorts price signals, without addressing the main issue of concern.

3. Creation of credit money by banks is not directly controlled or regulated by the central bank; there is no regulation mechanism in place whatsoever, except perhaps moral suasion.

4. The use of funds of this credit money is also not controlled or regulated. The two together (credit money creation + then using this money to fund asset purchases), have the greatest impact on excess variances in the business cycle.

So, in summary, you can take <u>your own</u> punch bowl away if you want. Banks won't care very much. They are still going to keep partying with the 1% if the future they see seems bright. As you know, you cannot take <u>their</u> punch bowl away; the decision to drink or not has been granted to them, since they create most of the money in an economy.

*You cannot force them to stop drinking, just like you cannot force them later to start drinking again.*

The last decades have shown this to us clearly. What you do with your little punch bowl is weakly correlated with whether bankers want to party.

Following the Tech Bust in 2000 and the Great Financial Crisis in 2008, policymakers employed the punch bowl strategy: they reduced the cost of money and made a lot more money available. The idea was that this money would make its way into the real economy, through the banks.

---

65 Sure, changing the interest rate does have some impact throughout the economy, particularly at the margins. But, it is still a smaller part of the funding mix for banks. The central bank assumption that everyone is drinking from the same punch bowl is *inconsistent with reality* and it consequently assumes a greater efficacy for monetary policy than really exists.

Take a look at the graph below. Did that help?

### US Loans as a % of total US bank assets (historic)

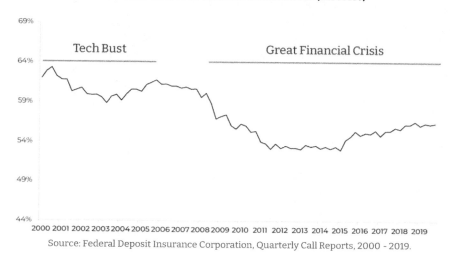

Source: Federal Deposit Insurance Corporation, Quarterly Call Reports, 2000 - 2019.

The psychology of banks is not mysterious; they act like you and me. If the future is uncertain, they keep their money close. If you have just had a financial hit, you work on damage repair. You don't go out and spend again, regardless of whether interest rates have dropped. If someone throws some cheap money your way, you put your own house in order first before you start to make investments again.

Even worse than not being able to take the banks' punch bowl away, you cannot control what they do when they are drunk on the punch. If bankers want to lend on the hope of ever-increasing asset prices (because the asset values are "tangible"), there is nothing regulators can do under the present system.

**In summary.**

This is our modern fractional reserve banking system. It is not at all capitalist; it is more like a closed, medieval guild system and it will always foster inequality and exclude out-groups by its very nature. It is as destructive as it is dishonest. It is about as far away from the concept of value, and from our better human values, as you can get.

## Takeaways

1. Banks' ability to create money essentially has allowed a form of what economists call "elite capture" to exist in the commercial banking sector.

2. The combination of commercial banks + the central bank + select politicians determine the rules for the banking sector, including setting the price of money in the economy and permitting banks to create their own money. None of this based on capitalism. The core of the banking sector does not function on free-market principles. It functions for the 1%.

3. There is almost no regulation whatsoever of the two most important aspects of banking: money creation and use of funds (how banks invest their money). Access to this money allows the 1% to capture vast amounts of wealth and influence in society and perpetuate their position.

4. These two factors: money creation + use of funds (particularly into asset financing) explain most of the excess variance in the business cycle (booms and busts).

5. Monetary policy is almost completely ineffective.

## Some thoughts:

- In the 2008 financial crisis in the United States, both left-wing and right-wing administrations took the same actions: they focused on saving the 1% the banks above all else. Same thing globally.

- The banks make ~~payments~~ contributions to both parties, in relatively equal measure.

- Booms and busts happen randomly, but regularly. For the past several hundred years. So, obviously, regulation and policy that ignore bank money creation don't work very well.

# 8
# WHO ENABLES THE ENABLERS?

To understand the 1% and their banking system, you need to know about a bank in Basel, Switzerland. Some of it starts to sound a bit like fiction, but I only touch on the (boring) economic facts.

**The Bank for International Settlements.**

The Bank for International Settlements (BIS) was set up by in the 1930s by eight countries. It is headquartered in Basel, Switzerland, although the bank's offices are, by international treaty, outside of Swiss jurisdiction. During the 1930s, the bank was criticised for acting to the benefit of Germany's Nazi government, and senior Nazis sat on the board of the bank. The BIS is described *as the central bank for the world's largest central banks* and holds regular, secret meetings in Basel for its members. [66]

To assist with creating confidence amongst banks, a committee under the supervision of the BIS has established rules for how much capital banks should hold, informally called the Basel Accords. Basel I was put in place in 1988 and suggested that banks hold 8% of their risk-weighted capital as reserves. I'm sure you are thinking: wow, 8% at the bottom of the inverted house of cards!! That ought to give everyone a lot of confidence.

Then, after that didn't have any observable effect whatsoever on financial

---

[66] If you are worried that I'm going to start to veer towards some weird conspiracy theories and are tempted to stop reading, don't. The BIS sounds like something out of a Dan Brown novel, but I cannot help it; these are just the facts. For full disclosure, I have not read conspiracy books about the BIS, like The Tower of Basel, although a friend here in Switzerland told me that the book existed. Personally, I'm not so interested in such things; I'm just interested in economics and banking. I don't think that the BIS or other central banks are involved in some vast conspiracy … mainly because they are just so completely ineffective in their day jobs that I cannot see them pulling it off.

crises, or their transmission amongst banks, or anything else, Basel II was put in place in <u>2004</u>. Basel II was more complex: some of the finest minds in economics, many of whom are household names and regularly appear on financial television and at Davos, helped devise a "Three Pillars" approach to managing fractional reserve banks. This was based on:

1. Minimum Capital Requirements, which moved away from a standardised reserves approach to something more customised, which could be created by each bank as they saw fit;

2. Supervisory Review, which give regulators "better tools" than previously available; and

3. Market Discipline, which contained a set of disclosure requirements so that banks could not hide toxic liabilities on their books.

And ... Basel II worked really well. There has been no excess variance in the business cycle since 2004. Stable prices. Full employment. No near bank failures. No liabilities hidden by banks. No global systemic risk events. Monetary policy achieved its goals. The central banks' crystal balls are great predictors of the future.

I'm just kidding. It was a total disaster, as you probably know from the 2008 financial crisis, the effects of which are still with us today. If you really understand banks, you get a little sarcastic about the system.

**Divination class time for central banks**

There is also a Basel III. I'll spare you the details. It was supposed to be implemented in stages by 2015. However, it has been repeatedly deferred, now until <u>2022</u>. Don't look it up: it is designed to be complex and opaque for outsiders. If you do spend time researching it, at least three things will keep you up at night: fractional reserve requirements are, well, a fraction; banks use their own internal risk models for many of the evaluations; and, much credit risk analysis is done by S&P and Moody's (you might recall that their business model is that banks pay for the credit assessments from these two, which is unlikely to lead to any conflict of interest; they are also the ones who brought you hundreds of AAA rated sub-prime mortgage vehicles). There are a lot of buzz words about macro-prudential regulation. Probably Basel III will be just as effective as the other accords.

The Basel Accords are not really enforced anywhere, except in the European Union. They are somewhat enshrined in law in the EU and overseen by the European Central Bank. The Basel Accords have, thankfully, prevented any problems in the fractional reserve banking systems of member states and, in particular, the banking systems of Portugal, Italy, Ireland, Greece and Spain have been doing really well over the past decade.

The ECB, under the transparent leadership of the Italians and the French, and despite printing more money than existed on Earth a few decades ago, most of which has been revealed to the European people in a completely forthright manner, is also doing super well.

The thing about the Basel Accords that is strange is that there is no mention anywhere in the thousands of pages of reports and recommendations of ~~the 1%~~ banks creating money. The mystery again; why do you think that is?

The Basel Accords seek to regulate banks as if money were created only by the central bank and then there was a money multiplier effect based on the reserve ratio (you remember that crucial ratio, the one that Canada, Australia, Sweden, the UK, etc. don't have) and/or as if banks were simply financial intermediaries, the Walt Disney version of what banks are all about.

None of these accords consider the implications at all of bank credit money creation

Here is the best way to understand the Basel Accords:

*The global regulatory system fails entirely to regulate the main source of funds, self-created credit money, for a bank.*

*The regulation also fails to control a key use of funds, into asset purchases, which is the main cause of excess variance in the business cycle.*

Other than these issues, there is nothing to worry about.

Combined with what you now know about banks' ability to influence their own capital, you might conclude that the Basel Accords are a complete fallacy.

## Takeaways

1. Don't be concerned that your local regulation of banks and money is ineffective. It is also completely ineffective at a global level.

2. That is because the 1% and the banks have captured regulators everywhere.

3. In terms of recessions/depressions/economic disasters, there is nothing standing between you and the same extreme variance in the economic cycles that have always hurt people in the past. Nothing. Don't expect that there is some regulator somewhere thinking about your best interests.

4. There have been 18 recessions in the past 100 years. Under the factional reserve banking system controlled by the 1%, events like the 2008 financial crisis and its aftermaths will always occur, to various degrees.

5. The Bank for International Settlements enables the 1%, globally. Their main role is to protect the interests of the 1%.

# 9
# WHO WILL PROTECT US AGAINST FUTURE ECONOMIC CRISES?

To answer this question, it is best to analyse whether we have learned from the cause of past crises. Those who enable the 1%, the central bankers and economists: do they understand the past so they can protect society from future recessions? OK, so you recall the recession chart over the past 100 years, so you can probably guess the answer. But, let's get into the mainstream economists' view briefly.

**Mainstream economists.**

Economists go by several different labels. However, most share the same things in common, such as believing that banks are simply financial intermediaries, mainly excluding the banking function from their economic models, and never having worked in a bank. Almost none of these mainstream economists will admit that commercial banks create the vast majority of money in an economy.

These economists all have a strong view on the importance of monetary policy. As an aside, if you sometimes cannot recall what monetary policy means, just keep in mind M for Magic. This is where a government politburo of elite economists sets the price of money in our free-market economy, based on predictions from their crystal ball.

Almost all mainstream economists are followers of J.M. Keynes, a British economist.[67] In general, Keynesian economics is simple to understand. It

---

67 Actually, he wasn't an economist; he had an undergraduate degree in mathematics, but he took one course in economics while at university. Then, he was a bureaucrat and a member of the

proposes that the government is the solution. Guess who likes Keynesian economics the most?

When the inverted house of cards that is the fractional reserve banking system collapses (as it does regularly), Keynes suggested that the government intervene in the economy. What happens when banks create money that is then used to fund asset purchases which (when asset prices reset to a more natural level) then blows up, destroying the money created? Well, for the Keynesian, that is a problem of ~~the intrinsically risky nature of fractional reserve banking the greed of the 1%~~ aggregate demand. So, as an intellectual justification, the government should step in and bail out the banks (who are, of course, just helpful actors in the economy) ... and thereby, the 1%, and spend more taxpayer money on increasing demand. That fixes everything.

Here is an example of one such economist, Jeffrey Sachs, who has been a professor at Harvard and Columbia and has written a textbook on macroeconomics.

This is what he had to say in regard to the causes of the Great Depression, in critique of the works of F.A. Hayek.

*"Hayek was wrong to think in the catastrophic depths of the Great Depression of the 1930s that all that was happening was an unwinding of the mal investment that had come from a credit boom. Clearly, there was a calamitous collapse of the banking sector, that had nothing to do with the earlier so-called mal investment."*[68]

I mean, you just want to laugh at this as it seems like such a joke to think that the collapse of the banking sector had "nothing to do" with earlier mal investment by banks in asset lending, like against stock values. You want to laugh until you realise that almost all mainstream economists think the same

establishment. He wrote economics textbooks based on the real world experience he gained as a government employee.

68 British Broadcasting Corporation, *Masters of Money*, Part 2, published 29 August 2016, from minute 23:36.

thing. You can get a quote from almost all household names in economics where they take the same position.

Almost all of them also take the same view in regard to the 2008 financial crisis: mal investment in asset lending, like against real estate values, had nothing to do with the near collapse of the banking sector. Banks are just helpful financial intermediaries. They don't create money. No impact on banks when this "money" is destroyed by loan (their asset) shortfalls. Maybe in Fantasyland.

So, with economists like this in charge of central banks, writing textbooks, and teaching the brightest minds of the next generation of economists, we don't have to worry about any repeat of past economic failures. Clearly, we have learned all of the lessons necessary in regard to the dangers of fractional reserve banking.

**Takeaways**

1. Many mainstream economists, in general, know less about the core of banking than you do, by this point in the book.
2. Those that really do understand that banks create money rarely speak up.
3. These economists, who lead central banks, do not appreciate the depth of banks' role in investing in the economy, particularly the harmful effect of asset lending.
4. The answer to the chapter question is: no one.

# 10
# ALIENS EVALUATE OUR MONEY

The aliens selling us the cure for cancer have a decision to make: what do they take in return? It depends on where they want to spend what they get in exchange.

If they want to take it home, all of our "money" is worthless to them; money has no intrinsic value, except in that it gives you purchasing power. Back home, no one takes US dollars, gold or bitcoin. So, if they want to take something home, they just need to propose something that we have. Nothing in the world has a single price; *all prices are just a ratio of two values*. Let's imagine that they fall in love with the statue *La Pietà* by Michelangelo. So, the price for the exchange is cancer drug : La Pietà. That is barter. Sometimes simple is best.

Now, however, suppose that they might want to buy a lot of stuff here on Earth, so they want to sell the cancer drug for money, which they can spend here. We give them three options: US dollars, gold or bitcoin. They investigate and then give us the answers below.

**US dollars.**

OK, so this is your world's reserve currency. It has a built-in mechanism where it loses a little bit of purchasing power every day, called inflation. It is better called a theft index. So, it innately encourages people to spend their money, rather than save it, which is bad for your civilisation, especially the poorest amongst you (although we see that you don't seem to give bank accounts to poor people so they can save. And, why should your banks do that, anyway? It isn't like they receive any benefits from society, so why should they give benefits?). The system is also fundamentally dishonest: you all pretend that you have money safely in the bank and yet it isn't your money and it cannot both be in the bank and, at the same time, loaned out by the bank. And, why does the world use it as a reserve currency and yet it is entirely tied to the performance of only one economy and under the control of their government (for a minority of money creation) and their banks (for a majority of the money creation)? The aliens conclude that US dollars are a poor store of value and that our banking system is dishonest and intrinsically biased against out-groups, which they consider immoral. So, they don't want this kind of money.

### Gold.

Next, they consider gold. OK, now we understand why you have an advanced civilisation and yet still use pieces of metal as symbols of value. That is why you waste your time with the costs of mining: your traditional banking system and your money are so dangerous and dishonest that you are driven to seek this alternative. Gold has a slowly increasing supply and therefore is superior to US dollars, as a store of value, since dollars are created without limit. They ask around to see who accepts gold as payment. Well, almost no one does. So, they don't want this kind of money either.

### Bitcoin.

Next, they consider bitcoin. This is more like it: it is highly secure, based on mathematical formulas, so it cannot be copied and you don't just need to trust human beings to do the right thing each time you use it. You can exchange it directly amongst people, like sending information, without going through a central switchboard. Transfers cost a small fraction of what it costs in dollars and they settle almost instantaneously, not in days or weeks. It has a fixed supply, so, by definition, is a superior store of value than dollars or gold. As with gold, that is why millions of you go to the expense of securing the crypto system: your banking and money system are so inferior in comparison. OK, they ask themselves, but why hasn't this crypto system, which seems so much more in line with your human values of freedom and fairness, why has it not replaced the banking and money system run by the 1%? Why does bitcoin only mainly function outside of your real economy?

### The decision.

The aliens reflect on the money options for a nanosecond, then they take the statue and go home. Undoubtedly, they feel a little sorry for us, in the same way we might feel sorry for the ancient Romans who were slowly poisoning themselves with trace amounts of lead in their everyday drinking water, without really knowing what was affecting their lives.

Before they leave, the aliens leave us a copy of Aleksandr Solzhenitsyn's *The Gulag Archipelago*. The message from this volume of books, they say, is that immoral control societies do not arise just from a small group of people. Everyone in a society contributes to the malaise, in their own small way, by telling or supporting lies.

**Takeaways**

1.   Almost everything on our planet is improving.
2.   Except the banking system.
3.   It would be a little embarrassing to have to explain our money to aliens.

# 11
# WHAT THE 1% FEARS THE MOST

Tired of not getting a fair deal in life? Not sure why the banks and the 1% get to use your money to generate high returns and you get little interest on your savings? Tired of fighting for your out-group and getting nowhere? Well, I have news for you: get used to it. Marches, pressure on politicians, occupying places, organising: all of this fails to address the underlying rottenness of a financial system that is controlled by the 1%. You think your out-group is ever going to get the same preferential credit evaluation for accessing money? Not in a fractional reserve banking system. Sure, they will throw you some crumbs now and then. There will be all of the right signals sent through marketing. But most people are never getting inside the guild.

Of course, you should also do all of the basics, like studying and working hard, being honest and disciplined and conscientious, and not adopting a victim mindset. You should get your own house in order. I'm not talking about the basics. After doing the basics, what you might ask yourself is: how can people lead a better life in a world so influenced by the 1%? Where they control the banking system, can print money, and are enabled by establishment institutions.

Here is what the 1% fears the most: *that the 99% become educated.* If you have read this far, you know about what enables them: money and fractional reserve banking. I think that there are two options for reducing the malignant effect of the 1% and their banks and making the world a better place: reform or adopt the crypto system. I set them out, in summary.

**Impact**.

One could cite numerous examples of the negative impact of the current banking system on society. Little things like, it is 2019 and half of humanity doesn't have access to the financial system or that many banks, where the poor do have access to banking, prey on them and keep them in a permanent state of debt dependency. Or that the 1% capture the vast majority of bank profits, while using depositors' money to help generate a lot of those profits. Or that thousands lose their jobs, savings, houses, etc. every decade or so because of bank-caused excess variance in the economic cycle.

Let's have a look at another mystery: where have lower and middle class incomes gone over the past 70 years?

**Value-add of the finance and insurance sectors in the US (% of GDP)** [69]

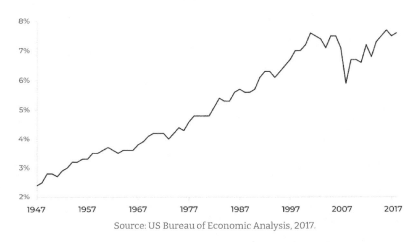

Source: US Bureau of Economic Analysis, 2017.

This graph shows that the role in the economy played by the financial sector has *quadrupled* since the end of the Second World War. Certainly, employment in the financial sector and wages paid to the financial sector have increased enormously. There is no question that shareholders in the financial sector (like the 1%) receive a substantial, and ever-increasing, chunk of GDP from banking.

But, "value-add"? How is "value-add" calculated? Well, a number of studies suggest that the numbers simply reflect increased risk taking in the sector, which is not a value-add to the economy. Other studies suggest that the value of financial intermediation is significantly overstated in national accounts.

There are other, rather important, calculations missing in the national accounts, like: that the cost of the economy regularly blowing up, caused by the financial sector and the 1%, are not included. Neither is the cost of government

---

69 You can question the composition of the numbers, of course. For example, the figures include insurance and other financial institutions that do not create money. The overall picture is sufficiently convincing to support the conclusion, though, in my view.

deposit insurance deducted from the "value-add" by the banks. (Actually, technically, that is perhaps right, as banks don't pay this cost and such insurance doesn't really exist, but it depends how you want to look at the illusion).

For about two decades after WWII, the percentage of financial sector profits to total profits in the economy was about 1.5%. This decade, it was as high as 15%.

But, wait a minute, I thought that banks were just helpful intermediaries, channeling surplus capital to those who need it. So, if this is the case, why would their role in the economy be so large, and growing?

If you know about financial markets, here is another example of why the story that the 1% and their enablers try to tell us is false: the way banks trade in the stock market is highly sensitive to economic performance. Just like builders, retailers, automotive stocks, etc. They don't trade as defensives. That is because, as you now know, banks are really investment companies, substantially to the benefit of the 1%. If banks were just helpful intermediaries, they would be priced more like utilities.

### The Fading American Dream
**Percent of Children Earning More than their Parents, by Year of Birth)**

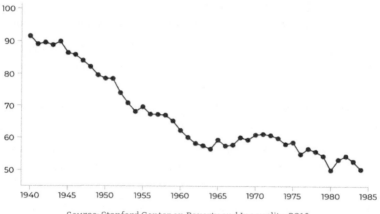

Source: Stanford Center on Poverty and Inequality, 2016.

What does this chart tell you?

Well, it tells you that lower and middle class income has been declining over the same period. It is similar in most developed countries.

There are also lots of studies that you can find that show declining lower and middle class wage growth over this period.

When you put the two charts on top of each other, you have a clue as to where lower and middle class income has gone over the past decades. It has gone (partially) to the financial sector. It has also gone to other areas, like globalisation (which the banks and 1% benefit enormously from), but a large part of the American Dream has been taken by banks. By the 1%.

**Change in real annual household capital income, by income group, 1979–2010**

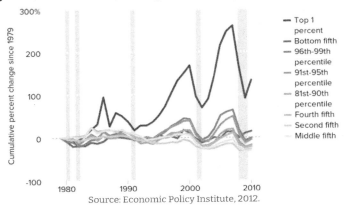

Source: Economic Policy Institute, 2012.

What does this chart tell you?

Well, it tells you that the 1% are capturing a significant and increasing share of the wealth in the economy, aided by their control of the banking sector.

You want a few examples of the 1%? Probably the top two members of the 1%, who particularly benefit from the banking system, are Jamie Dimon and Warren Buffett.

Jamie Dimon is CEO of JP Morgan and its second largest individual shareholder.

Warren Buffet has made a meaningful part of his fortune by investing in the financial sector. As of the most recent filing for Berkshire Hathaway, 7 of his 10 largest holdings were in banks or relations/enablers. [70]

They both enormously benefit from the fact that the banking sector takes a little bit from everyone to accumulate enormous wealth at the top.

---

70 Holdings in top 10: 2. Bank of America 3. Wells Fargo 6. American Express 7. US Bancorp 8. Moody's 9. Goldman Sachs 10. JP Morgan. Source: Q3 2018 SEC filing.

**Reform.**

There is a book by John Grisham called *The Firm*, where the main character is hard-working and smart and he puts in the effort to figure out something that seemed wrong to him. After doing some research, he realised that the firm was owned by the Mafia. You are now that guy.

Maybe proposing reform will work, but I doubt it. The 1% and their banking system are just so entrenched in society that it is hard to imagine really changing it. In addition, the fractional reserve banking system is so flawed that it is hard to know where to start with reform. Certainly (mainly cosmetic) reforms have been put in place over the years, with no effect on failures in the economic system and no reduction in the power of the 1% and no impact on inequality. The system also relies on innate human biases that are simply hard to remove. Further, technologically, the banking system is an analog type system: not well-suited for the 21st century. Some parts of it are really obsolete from a technical perspective and simply cannot be upgraded.

There are certainly some key reforms that should happen. I set out some of them below.

1. Banks should not be allowed to create their own money.
2. Uses of funds for lending to asset projects should be regulated.
3. Banks should pay for government deposit insurance.
4. Government deposit insurance should really be made into insurance, not just printing money.
5. Politicians should not be allowed to take contributions from banks.
6. etc. Yeah, I know, "Duh".

In my view, reform is not the optimal way to spend time and resources, for the reasons set out below.

- The fight would be extremely difficult, against a motivated adversary with significant resources; the risk/reward pay-off isn't compelling.
- Reform is possible, but it would always be in the context of an overall money and banking model that is flawed; it is inherently dishonest and its structure is based on the inverted house of cards arrangement by its very nature.
- There might be a better alternative.

**The crypto system.**

Before we get into what the crypto system is, and before you freak out, let's go over what it isn't.

**It isn't for drug dealers.**

In the early days of the internet, many people had older relatives who listened disapprovingly to them talking about "that internet thing" and declared that the internet was mainly about pornography and that the only people who would use it would be perverts. I presume that you use the internet now and then and that you don't consider yourself a pervert.

The same mindset is true today for the crypto system. If you want to buy drugs you are much better off doing that with money that is anonymous, like US dollars in cash. Same with money-laundering: the crypto system is based on an unchangeable record book and radical transparency. Yes, accounts are confidential, just like your bank account, but users can be identified, by technology and inference. If you were a criminal and know technology and are smart, you would never use the crypto system for drugs or to launder money.

**It isn't a fraud or a scam.**

Jamie Dimon and Warren Buffett will tell you, with a straight face, that the crypto system is about printing money that does not have any intrinsic worth. Now you know the truth about how banks operate, so you won't be deceived by them. You should also know that the crypto system is an *existential threat* to the fractional reserve banking system.

So, asking these two guys what they think about the crypto system is like asking a taxi driver what he thinks about Uber. The fact is that the core of the banking system is based on a lie and deception, which enables the 1%. You make your own mind up about whether this system might be termed a "fraud" or a "scam".

**It isn't complicated to understand.**

The banking system is a lot more complicated. So complicated, in fact, that it takes a little bit of our money every day without us really noticing. So complicated that it holds us back from living a full life, contributes to inequality, and subjects us all occasionally to dangerous economic risks.

**Here is what it is.**

In 2009 Satoshi Nakamoto created a system of money that corresponds to how humanity has exchanged value for most of our history. Technologically, this system is based on mathematical formulae and a straight-forward verification and record system. The implications are *spectacular:* you can now trust exchanging value with another person or institution <u>directly,</u>

globally, even if you don't know them.

The crypto system is profoundly natural, a very human invention, based on the concepts of *freedom* and *fairness*. It is the most authentic form of money that society has had since indications of value were part of our memory.

It is characterised as set out below.

- Based only on PV money (i.e. value that exists today, not tied to any required future value creation).
- Allows value to be exchanged directly between two parties <u>without any middleman</u>, almost instantaneously and at extremely low cost.

A better description than the term crypto currencies is *honest money*. This money system is about more than just exchanging value; it is also about our values.

The crypto system is digital technology to banking and paper money's analog technology. The potential, the combination of value and values, that this new (old really) system unlocks for humanity is hard to overstate.

The table below summarises the difference between the fractional reserve banking system and the crypto system.

| Function | Traditional banking system | Crypto system |
| --- | --- | --- |
| Value capture | Bank shareholders, senior management | Owned by all participants |
| Ability to create money | Yes, unlimited | No, fixed supply |
| Currencies as standard of value | Poor, lots of currencies, all tied to nation states | Poor, global (good), but lack of depth, lack of link to real economy |
| Currencies as store of value | Poor store of value (unlimited supply) | Good store of value (fixed supply)<br>Will be enhanced by depth |
| Payment system | Expensive, slow settlement, rapid point of sale, inefficient | Transaction time much slower than traditional, direct between users, low transaction fees, quick settlement |
| Ownership of deposited funds | Owned by the bank | Owned and controlled only by users |
| Profit driven by deposit-loan mis-match | Yes | No |
| Authority | Nation state government | Global community, fixed supply mechanism |
| Trust | Single, centralised body: bank (including their servers, employees) | Based on mathematical proofs; open, community verification |
| Organisational structure | Highly centralised | Distributed, based on the community |
| Links to the real economy | High; strong links | Almost non-existent |

The crypto system threatens nation state currency as well as the fractional reserve banking system and the 1%. It is *incompatible* with fractional reserve banking. The crypto system is based on a transparent record of truth, captured forever in a giant record book, and on value that exists today.

The fractional reserve banking system is intrinsically dishonest: bankers will tell you that your money is both safely in the bank and, at the same time, they are lending it out to others. They will tell you that it is your money while, legally, it belongs to the bank and they can do what they want with it. And, they keep most of the profits from banking, from using your money.

The crypto system takes the money creation power out of the hands of the middlemen, the 1% and their banking system. *Without the power to create money and control who gets to use it and on what terms, the influence behind the 1% will diminish.* The rotten influence related to money and its preservation of the current 1% dominated system will diminish. The institutionalised preference for in-groups that is intrinsic to the current banking system can only be removed if you remove the institutions: the middlemen. The vast profits captured by these middlemen are largely unjustified by the riskiness of their core business, if done on a matched deposit-loan basis; the crypto system mainly removes the need for the middlemen, allowing profits to flow to their rightful owners, the depositors.

This will result in a significantly greater sharing of the wealth created by productive opportunities in the economy; *the 99% will become economically much better off under this model.* Crypto is the money for the 99%.

If you want to make the world a better place, you need to start with money: how it is created and allocated in society. Only the crypto system has the ability to take the money creation power away from the 1% and their banking system. Only the crypto system can lead to greater wealth gain by the 99% and reduction of inequality in society.

Only one of these two systems can survive. They cannot co-exist together in the long-term.

### What exactly are crypto currencies?

Crypto currencies are money, just like US dollars or gold and are easy to understand. They differ from US dollars in these ways:

- They cannot be censored by a bank or government; no one can access your account except you. You hold the password to your crypto currency account (called a private key, which is just a long password).

- They are a direct network, so you can send money by yourself to anyone you want. You make the transfer yourself, like sending an email. It happens almost instantaneously and costs almost nothing; it is like sending information. With the banking system, you have to ask your bank to send it and it costs, relatively, a lot of money and takes several days to clear. With the payments industry (credit cards), technically you give the merchant permission to *pull* money from your account; this involves about 20 players in the chain and is costly and very insecure. With crypto currencies, it is a *push* system; it involves just you and the recipient, costs nothing, and is extremely secure.

## What is a blockchain?

Blockchain is also simple to understand: it is just the architecture that underlies the crypto currency and provides security and administration functions.

*Administration:* all transactions are recorded in a giant, transparent record-book, for everyone to see (names and amounts in the accounts are confidential, of course).

*Security:* blockchain uses mathematical formulae and a straight-forward verification process to make sure that all transactions are valid (e.g. eliminates fraud, you cannot send the same money to several people, etc.).

As an analogy: the traditional banking system, central banks, payment networks, etc. are the architecture on which nation state (fiat) money runs.

Crypto currency networks are vastly more efficient technologically. It is like comparing a smart phone to an old-fashioned fixed line telephone system with manual switchboard operators.

It is true that some blockchains use a fair bit of electricity (although much of it is renewable and would not otherwise be utilised); it isn't magically free. To make a comparison with the traditional system, imagine adding up the costs, globally, for how much banks spend on administration and security? It would be a vast amount; the crypto expense is a small fraction of these costs. Other blockchains use very little electricity. As the industry matures and the technology evolves, these costs are expected to come down.

You could get into the programming and mathematical details of how the blockchain architecture works, just like you could learn exactly how your car works or how the internet works. But, it isn't necessary to know this to use crypto currency (or your car or the internet).

## What will cause the crypto system to be more widely adopted?

The biggest problem facing the crypto system is its lack of connection to the real economy; this is caused partly by the opposition from the 1% and the banking system. A link to goods and services, whether in the form of purchases or as a use of excess capital (savings) is the main missing piece of the crypto system. This comes from the fact that there is no crypto banking system yet.

This is illustrated in the form of a puzzle, below.

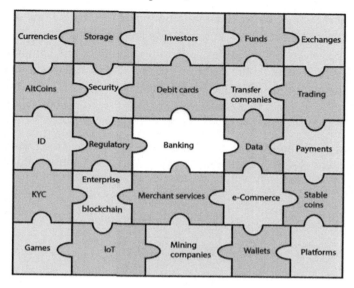

Obviously, a link to the real economy is fundamental to any financial system and this is the main impediment holding back the entire crypto industry.

By bank system, I mean that holders of crypto currencies need to have the option to link their savings, a store of their value, to productive opportunities in the real economy. When this issue is resolved, it will significantly spur crypto adoption. Real crypto banking will be the Netflix moment for the entire crypto space. This will drive the future value of crypto currencies and many existing crypto firms.

**Takeaways**

1.  The 1% are vampires. They, and their banking system, live off of you being ignorant and having no alternatives.

2.  The increasing capture of larger amounts of GDP by the financial sector (and the 1%) is correlated with declining lower and middle class incomes.

3.  One option to challenge the 1% is to try to reform the banking system. However, it would still need to be accepted that the model underlying fractional reserve banking is flawed and dishonest.

4.  The other option is to increasingly adopt the crypto system. This is an existential threat to the 1% and their banking system.

5.  The biggest impediment to the widespread adoption of the crypto system is the lack of a banking model for crypto. This is one of the main reasons that crypto currencies price like assets rather than currencies.

# 12
# THE FINANCIAL SYSTEM AND YOUR SEX LIFE

The failure by Stripe to provide services to OMGYes, a site that provides education in relation to women's sexual pleasure, illustrates one of the problems with the 1% controlled banking system: they control your freedom to make decisions in life, even in small ways. It also shows the difference between fintech and crypto. Fintech is the cool, slightly hippie version of the traditional financial system. But ... it is still the traditional financial system.

The Collison brothers from Limerick, Ireland who created Stripe seem to personify fintech: incredibly intelligent, disruptive, well-intentioned billionaires. Despite personally wanting to fund OMGYes, the traditional financial system that controls Stripe said no. The crypto system is fundamentally different: there is no middleman to tell you what you can do with your money (as long as it is legal, of course). No government, no bank. The decision is up to you. Payments go from you to the recipient.

Economists use the term "repugnance" to describe activities that have a moral element to them. Many banks and financial intermediaries do not allow their customers to make purchases they deem repugnant, even if they are legal. A good example is provided by the fintech company, Stripe, which facilitates payments.

Here is an excerpt from their website:

*"Why can't we work with some businesses?*
*Behind the scenes, we work closely with payment networks (such as Visa and*
*Mastercard) and banking partners across more than two dozen countries.*
*Each institution has strict legal regulations that govern them and specific*
*rules about the types of businesses they do and do not work with."*[71]

One such business they declined to provide financial services for is OMGYes.
Here is what Stripe had to say about why they declined to provide services to
OMGYes:

*"The business approached us and we were eager to work with them, but after*
*a month of deliberations, our financial partners did not agree. Instead,*
*because the website has explicit tutorials, it still falls under the umbrella of*
*unsupportable businesses. While we were not able to persuade our financial*
*partners this time around, we will continue to holistically look at and*
*advocate for businesses that sell adult products and services."*

One the one hand, you could perhaps say: well, they wanted to do the right
thing. On the other hand, you might say: well, the result is that they didn't do
what they felt was the right thing. The traditional financial system just doesn't
allow it. You might also say: if it is my money and it is legal, why does some
financial services company decide for me what is morally acceptable or not?

71 Danika Lyon, Industry Relations, Stripe Inc. "Why some businesses aren't allowed." 12 August 2016.
As sourced from: Al Roth economics blog, guest post by Stephanie Hurder. 28 August 2018.

Using terms like "holistically" and "advocating for businesses" doesn't change the fact that they said **OMGNo** to **OMGYes**. [72]

Finally, here is what Stripe says,

*"As a result, the decision to support a business is not solely up to Stripe; it involves the various financial companies in the credit card processing chain."*

You want to know what the difference is between the traditional banking system, including "fintech" companies like Stripe, and the crypto system? Well, here it is:

*In the crypto system, the decision to support a business is solely up to you.*

It is your money and it is your moral value judgement.

In the future, people will decide what is morally repugnant to them and what is not. Increasingly, they will decide that the 1% and their banks are what is repugnant.

**Takeaways**

1.  Our current banking system was not created with the ideas of freedom or fairness in mind. It was designed for control.
2.  Fractional reserve banking is bad for your sex life.

---

72 Of course, even if it doesn't change the end result or the fact that it contributes to enabling the traditional financial system to decide morality for you (I know, what a joke), at least Stripe should get some credit for being open and honest about the decision process. You won't find many articles like this on bank websites that say: well, we would have liked to have provided services to this customer, but, you know, the traditional financial system finds education about women's sexual pleasure repugnant. Meanwhile, check out our financial services to strip mining companies in Africa, here ....

# 13
# KARL MARX AND THE 1%

Karl Marx knew more about the 1% and banking than the vast majority of people. Certainly, he had some deeper insights than most modern, mainstream economists. Is it possible that his knowledge of fractional reserve banking and money were the spark that led him, as a young idealist, to conclude that the capitalist system was unfair?

In retrospect, we can view Marx's writings and the communist experiment critically, through an historical lens. The results aren't that great: maybe over 100 million people dead, the aspirations of generations destroyed, almost everyone in their societies turned into liars and government informers. Perhaps Marx's disciples, enjoying eternity together in Hell, might be reflecting on that, in fact, they did stand to lose more than just their chains.

And yet ... people still read his works! This table shows the most frequently taught books by notable economists, in US universities (compiled by MarketWatch).

| Author | Most frequently taught work | Count | Teaching score |
|---|---|---|---|
| Karl Marx | The Communist Manifesto | 3189 | 99.7 |
| Adam Smith | Wealth of Nations | 1587 | 95.5 |
| Paul Krugman | Economics | 1081 | 89.4 |
| Gregory N. Mankiw | Macroeconomics | 989 | 87.5 |
| Thomas L. Friedman | The Lexus and the Olive Tree | 733 | 77.8 |
| Milton Friedman | Capitalism and Freedom | 556 | 65.7 |
| Joseph Stiglitz | Economics | 528 | 62.8 |
| John Maynard Keynes | The General Theory of Employment | 348 | 44.2 |
| Malcolm Gladwell | The Tipping Point: How Little Things Can Make a Big Difference | 225 | 28.7 |
| John Kenneth Galbraith | The Affluent Society | 177 | 22.5 |
| Michael Lewis | Moneyball: The Art of Winning an Unfair Game | 50 | 6.4 |
| Ben Bernanke | Nonmonetary Effects of the Financial Crisis in the Propagation of the Great Depression | 40 | 5.1 |
| Janet Yellen | Efficiency Wage Models of Unemployment | 31 | 3.9 |
| Nouriel Roubini | Crisis Economics: A Crash Course in the Future of Finance | 16 | 2 |
| Alan Greenspan | The Age of Turbulence: Adventures in a New World | 16 | 2 |

Source: Open Syllabus Project / MarketWatch analysis

The only two overall books assigned more frequently than *The Communist Manifesto* were some writing style guide and Plato's *Republic* (note: list excludes books like the Bible, US Constitution, etc.). Almost all of the French intelligentsia have communist sympathies, as do many mainstream economists in the UK. Thomas Piketty's *Capital in the Twenty-First Century* (a play on the wording of Marx's book, *Capital*), sold more than a million copies and was on the NY Times bestseller list. Paul Krugman called it "the most important economics book of the year, and maybe of the decade." Its main idea is that ... inequality is an inherent part of capitalism and can only be reversed through state interventionism. If this seems like *déjà vu* to you, as in: already read something like that, people already tried that, didn't work very well ... you can be forgiven.

Krugman, Piketty and other left-leaning economists must certainly be correct that income inequality is rising in the US and Europe. There are a number of ways to measure this and my own view is that Piketty's data, for what he labels r and g, just isn't very useful. There is a lot of error that goes into these two variables and he ignores wealth creation almost completely (which is, partly, access to money and banking and one of the secrets to success of the 1%). But, the trend is clearly towards increasing wealth concentration amongst the 1%. However, *it must be questioned whether this is "capitalism's" fault*. What cannot be questioned is how absurd the conclusions of most "communist sympathisers" are: more power to the state and higher tax. First, even in French there are history books about the failure of communist economics in Russia and China. Second, more importantly, now that you know about the banking guild, here is a rule of thumb when considering solutions to inequality: more state intervention = more power to the 1%. Third, how about being a little more innovative than just talking about more or less state intervention, or higher or lower tax? That discussion is a little passé. You know, it is the Twenty-First Century; what about a technology solution?

## Is capitalism to blame for inequality?

In some sense, yes. It is a harsh world and, consequently, the market can be a harsh place. Markets experience excesses. As Theodore Roosevelt showed us, there is unquestionably some role for government to protect people against the excess effects of markets.

More importantly, we need to define our terms. It is not useful to define capitalism just as "money"; that doesn't explain a system. More accurate is to define capitalism as the process where prices are set by the market mechanism. In this sense, (market-based) capitalism is certainly a contributor to inequality; that just reflects our biology.

However, performance in a market is a secondary aspect of inequality. More important is access to money and that has to come first in any undertaking; it doesn't arise naturally out of an economic process. Access to money and the banking system explains much more in relation to inequality in society than the effect of capitalism/markets.

Of course, access to money and banking on preferential terms is not a sufficient condition for someone to join or remain in the 1%. Society is relatively dynamic and intelligence and conscientiousness are highly correlated with success. Similarly, just because you had wealth in one generation is not a guarantee that it will endure forever. However, a significant, and obscured, reason for the inequality in society and the disproportionate influence of the 1% is the ability of banks to create money and the ability of the 1% to access this money. This money creation process and the system that enables it is an important source of power for the 1%.

Knowing what you now know, you will realise that *bank money creation is not at all based on competitive, free-market capitalism*. In fact, the banking system is better compared to an elitist guild that works for the benefit of in-groups. Other aspects of the money system, like the government committee that sets the price of money for everyone in society, are more like pure communism than anything else. Inequality arises from these mechanisms.

## Why this soft spot for Marx?

The positive feelings that many academics in the social sciences and economics feel towards Marx are somewhat hard to understand, on the surface. A good number of his economic theories turned out to be questionable. Keynes commented that Marxism was founded on a misunderstanding of Ricardo, which is funny and insulting at the same time. *Capital* is poorly structured and a hard read; I suspect that few economists have really read it (the same could be said for Keynes' *General Theory*). It seems pretty clear that lack of market price signals in communism resulted in an inefficient allocation of resources. Millions died. Life sucked. Eventually, Russia, China, etc. called off the experiment. It is hard to justify liking Marx and communism just from an intellectual or moral position.

So, why do so many smart, decent people have a soft spot for Marx? There are probably a number of reasons, but I think that one of them might be a feeling that the system is biased against the average person. That there is something inherently unfair about our economic model. A voice inside you that says something is causing an uneven playing field.

That might be right. In my view, the fractional reserve banking system is an inherent cause of inequality in our society. It is something almost intangible, hard to see clearly, a malignancy but one that mainly keeps to the background. It is the money for the 1%, an important source of their influence.

A problem for those with a soft spot for Marx is this: the fractional reserve banking system isn't really capitalistic. It doesn't function based on free markets. It is structured more like a guild.

Young Marx certainly seemed to know about banks and their connection to the 1%, perhaps from knowledge gained from his wealthy family and in- laws. In a harsh age, no doubt what he saw seemed immoral and unchangeable: the 1% had access to "fictitious" money via the banking system in a way that those who just sold their labour did not. While quality of life for most is vastly better today, one could wonder about the continuing impact of the fractional reserve banking system, which functions under the same model as in his day.

Here are some indications that Marx saw through the deception of the fractional reserve banking system.

*"The formation of a fictitious capital is called capitalisation."*[73]

*"With the development of interest-bearing capital and the credit system, all capital seems to double itself, and sometimes treble itself, by the various modes in which the same capital, or perhaps even the same claim on a debt, appears in different forms in different hands. The greater portion of this 'money-capital' is purely fictitious. All the deposits, with the exception of the reserve fund, are merely claims on the banker, which, however, never exists as deposits. To the extent that they serve in clearing-house transactions, they perform the function of capital for the bankers - after the latter have loaned them out. They pay one another their mutual drafts upon the non-existing deposits by balancing their mutual accounts."*[74]

[Referring to bankers and the banking system] *"For the entire vast extension of the credit system, and all credit in general, is exploited by them as their private capital. These fellows always possess capital and incomes in money-form or in direct claims on money. The accumulation of the wealth of this class may take place completely differently than actual accumulation, but it proves at any rate that this class pockets a good deal of the real accumulation."*[75]

## Is the crypto system for capitalists or communists?

The crypto system doesn't have a political ideology. It is simply an honest form of money.

It also cuts out the bank middleman and allows people to exchange value directly. In this sense, it involves a political value judgement: based on what you believe, do you want to support the fractional reserve banking system or not, if there is an alternative?

Some enthusiasts claim that the crypto system is about *freedom*. Well, it sure is. Who doesn't want that?

It is also about *fairness*. A large part of the crypto community talk about being motivated to make the world a better place, a place where the influence of the 1% and their banking system is reduced. For example, the UN's World Food Programme uses blockchain technology to provide identity and has distributed millions of dollars in food to tens of thousands of Syrian refugees in Jordan since May 2017. The major benefit to the food program so far is "a

73 K. Marx, *Capital: A Critique of Political Economy*, Moscow, Institute of Marxism-Leninism, 1959, p.334
74 Marx, *cit. op.* p.337.
75 Marx, *cit. op.* p.344.

large drop in payments to financial services firms", the usual middlemen for transactions. Such fees have dropped "significantly," according to Houman Haddad, the WFP executive leading the project. [76]

## Criticism from mainstream economists.

The crypto system has attracted criticism from some mainstream economists. Their objections and some commentary are set out below.

1.  *Not a good store of value.* This is true and false. Crypto currencies lack a connection to the real economy at the moment (mainly because banks and their enablers oppose crypto as an existential threat to them, partly because crypto has not developed many must-have products yet). So, it is true that crypto currencies are priced more like assets than currencies at the moment. Further, a related lack of market depth and few investment options for investors in the space contribute to mis-pricing. In the long run, if the crypto system develops a connection to the real economy, crypto currencies will be a superior store of value than nation state currencies because crypto currencies have fixed supply.

2.  *No intrinsic use.* This is false. Crypto currencies clearly meet the main criteria for money: they are scarce and are accepted as having purchasing power. A main use case is peer-to-peer exchange of value, which is in place today. More use cases will emerge as the crypto system links to the real economy.

3.  *Attracts fraudsters.* This is true. Perhaps it is like this with all new technologies, but it seems like it is our human nature to get overly enthusiastic about opportunities for progress. This was certainly the case with many inventions throughout history, from railroads to the internet. All attracted unsavoury characters seeking to sell a gullible public on unlikely schemes. However, it isn't widows and orphans who might get swindled in crypto. It is people who are at least experienced enough to set up and manage a wallet on the blockchain. Honestly, if you are smart enough to do that I don't think there is need for the government to act as a nanny towards your crypto investments.

4.  *Utility tokens are disguised securities* and should not have been issued. This is probably true for most companies.

5.  *Lots of people in crypto wear cat t-shirts* or cowboy hats or both, have

advanced degrees in the pure sciences, and seem to operate at 100 miles a minute. This is true. It is a bit of a culture clash with the economist elite. All things considered, the criticism from thoughtful mainstream economists (not the rabid ones, financed by the banks) does not change the positive, fundamental case for the crypto system. I believe that many mainstream economists would be more supportive of the crypto system if they took the time to understand its fundamentals and the solutions that it offers to real-world economic problems.

**Takeaways**

1. The only remnants of communist ideology, where the state sets prices, that persist today are to be found in North Korea and at the Federal Reserve (and other central banks around the world that set the price of money in an economy). Happily, it looks like North Korea might be changing for the better.

2. The 1% and their banking system probably make more people sympathetic towards communism than reading Karl Marx does.

3. The best way to reduce inequality in society is not communism or capitalism; it will be by reforming or replacing the fractional reserve banking system.

# 14
# HOW THE 1% SUCKS YOUR BLOOD EVERY TIME YOU MAKE A PAYMENT

Every time you use your money, you essentially pay a tax to the 1%. Let's learn why.

### Understanding push - pull.

The existing payment cards - banking system is based on pull technology, which is complex, costly and prone to fraud. The plumbing necessary for credit card payments, combined with the traditional banking industry, is illustrated below. Add another 5-8 steps for cross-border payments.

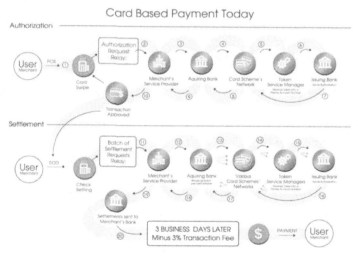

If it looks like it was cobbled together in a fit of absent-mindedness based on 1970s technology, that is because it was.

And what alternative do you have to using your credit card? Like taxation, it is essentially forced on you; there is no choice. And, the costs of the system are very high, spread amongst all consumers in a society.

There are two important things to realise about the structure of the credit card processor industry:

- it has a high break-even point;

- and a large number of self-interested, uncoordinated participants fighting for industry profits.

The main impetus for switching from credit cards to a new system payments will come from *merchants*. The average credit card processing cost for a retail business where cards are swiped is roughly 1.90% - 2.15% for Visa and Mastercard transactions. The average cost for card-not-present transactions, such as online, is roughly 2.30% - 2.50%.

Worse, long transaction reconciliation times have a negative impact on merchant's working capital. With credit cards, maybe you think you have paid for that latte right away, but the money reaches the merchant days later. The merchant also bears the risk of chargebacks for a considerable period of time after: typically for up to 90 - 120 calendar days (based on a "Central Site Business Date"). Chargeback costs to merchants is expected to reach $31 billion by 2020. [77] In 2016, only 23% of chargebacks were in relation to identity theft. So-called "friendly fraud" accounted for 28% and "chargeback fraud" accounted for another 28%. [78]

A key issue in the payments industry is security. With your credit card, you are not actually making a payment. What you are doing is giving an approval (based on your Personal Account Number) to the merchant to pull money from your account. Since the merchant is just the end link in the payments chain, the merchant's system needs to transmit your account details to every other entity in the process. So, you, the customer, effectively have to trust all of the 20 parties in this chain.

Payment processors biggest cost is security; they spend billions each year on trying to prevent fraud. Think maybe you were not affected? In 2017, the Identity Theft Resource Center counted 1,579 data breaches in the United States, up 45 percent from 2016, affecting 178,955,069 records. [79] Credit card

---

77 The Nilson Report, 2017

78 LexisNexis 2016 True Cost of Fraud study.

79 Note: only covers those data breaches notified by companies to authorities. Of these notified

fraud in the US exceeded $7 billion in 2017. [80] In the United Kingdom, 4.7 million people reported their credit card lost or stolen or misused, with an average loss per person of £833 pounds. [81] Financial institutions globally are expected to spend $9.2 billion by 2020 to prevent credit card fraud. [82]

The crypto payment system works based on push technology. This is illustrated below. [83]

In the crypto system, what keeps push payments from A to B (which could be individuals, or an individual to a merchant, or a business to a business) safe is straight-forward and based on:

Keeping your private keys (basically a long complex password) secure; and

The community working together, based on economic incentives to keep the system database protected.

All system users basically contribute a small amount to a diverse group of system supporters to ensure that it remains safe. The crypto system is mathematically almost impossible to break. There are some weak points (like exchanges, which are just SQL databases) but these are not part of the crypto system.

Unlike the 1%'s banking system, with the crypto system the merchant gets the money right away. With the push system, the crypto system, there are no chargebacks. In the crypto system, security costs are a tiny fraction of the amount spent by traditional players. To criticise the crypto system for excessive electricity costs is simply the big lie strategy: it isn't comparing the role the miners play in the system to the equivalent functions required in the fractional reserve banking and payments systems and by society. Losses in the genuine crypto system are almost non-existent, compared to an astronomical

breaches, 37% of notifications did not quantify the number of records - such as Social Security numbers and payment card data - that was exposed.
80 FT Partners Research and Statistica.
81 Report commissioned by Comparethemarket.com, for the last 12 months to July 2018.
82 Juniper Research, Online Payment Fraud: Key Vertical Strategies and Management 2015-16.
83 You could add some minor complexity, like wallet details or maybe Alice and Bob will use a form of a crypto bank in the future, but the heart of the push system in crypto is just this simple.

amount of money lost to payments fraud, because of the convoluted infrastructure and the pull technology.

Vitalik Buterin from Ethereum, who will be known as one of the greatest computer scientists of all time, has the annoying trait of being really honest and open about technical issues in the crypto system. In respect of payments, this is the scalability trilemma, which posits that (at the moment) a blockchain cannot have all three of these characteristics at the same time: decentralised, scalable, and secure; it can only have two of the three. It allows bank-funded economists to ignore the superiority of the crypto system over the fractional reserve banking system and the payments system and focus on issues important to them: the horrifying possibility of cold lattes, because payment times can sometimes take too long.

Being rude to Vitalik for slow processing [84] and concluding that the crypto system will never reach its potential is like yelling at Gordon Moore in the 1960s that there are not enough transistors on a microchip to do anything useful. First, tech scales exponentially; it is a bad idea to bet against that. Second, there are also many interim solutions. With a proper crypto bank, for example, the crypto bank could guarantee to the merchant the availability of funds immediately, even if it will take a few minutes after to settle on the blockchain. Third, the criticism applies to small payments where speed is important, but there is a vast market for larger payments where settlement could be in minutes, not seconds, and still be vastly superior to the present system. That is why crypto transfers will start at the larger end: payment for large shipments of coffee beans can take days to process through the banking system. In this part of the chain, commodity players would be ecstatic to wait 10 minutes for confirmation and finality.

84 From the latte buyer's, not the merchant's perspective.

**Takeaways**

1.  The biggest weakness in the payment system is security, which is vastly inferior to the crypto system.
2.  The only effective way to eliminate payment fraud almost entirely and the costs of trying to prevent this fraud is to adopt the crypto system.
3.  The crypto payment system, based on push technology, is simpler than pull technology and will replace the old system.
4.  A decade from now no one will use the pull-based system; it will completely disappear.
5.  Through the banking system, the 1% benefits from the vast amounts paid in credit card fees every year.

# 15
# THE FACE OF THE ENEMY

No man personifies being a supporter of the 1% and their banking system better than the head of the Bank for International Settlements. He will do everything he can to protect the fractional reserve banking system and prevent the 99% from learning about this key source of power for the 1%.

**The head of the BIS.**

If you want to put a face on the enemy, here he is: Augustin Carstens, head of the Bank for International Settlements, the central bank for the world's largest central banks, former politician, and former head of the central bank of Mexico.

A vocal (and completely unbiased) critic of the crypto system, here is what he had to say recently. [85]

*"Cryptocurrencies are ... a bubble, a Ponzi scheme and an environmental disaster."*

This is what you have to expect from those working for the 1%, the enablers of fractional reserve banking. It is an appropriate propaganda technique from the BIS: employ a "big lie" strategy to attack those who are beginning to stand against the 1%. The crypto system is a return to an earlier, more natural human system where money and value are clear to everyone, recorded forever in writing. Don't think that they are ignorant; they know that the crypto system is the only real alternative to their banking system.

The crypto system is exactly the opposite of a Ponzi scheme, which is based on deception and secrecy; indeed, it is simply a fact that the fractional reserve banking system has Ponzi scheme characteristics. The 2008 financial crisis, the collapse of the inverted house of cards that is the fractional reserve banking system, was the impetus for the creation of the crypto system: to counter institutional fraud and protect people from being preyed upon by the 1%.

The crypto system is an environmental disaster? A picture is worth a thousand words, so here is one for you to consider.

A tanker owned by the Mexican government's oil company, PEMEX, and financed by Augustin Carstens, burns in the Gulf of Mexico, 26 May 2015.

---

85 Interview with Basel Zeitung newspaper, 25 June 2018. Translated from the German. Dr Carstens holds a PhD in economics from the University of Chicago. He has recently been appointed to head the BIS and moved to Basel.

The "mining" function in a proof of work (PoW) crypto system uses electricity; much of this comes from renewable sources that are not otherwise utilised. PoW serves two basic functions: administration and security for the entire system. Imagine adding up the costs, globally, for how much banks spend on administration and security? It would be a vast amount; the crypto expense is a small fraction of these costs. In addition, as the crypto system allows for secure payment with finality, there are no enforcement costs required. So, for a fair comparison, add in the costs in the traditional system of lawyers, courts, police, auditors, regulators, etc. and then make the comparison.

The main (and only) report on crypto electricity use is not at all rigorous (it infers technical inputs from assumed financial outputs), the "researcher" has no background in energy economics or systems modelling, and the extremely high figures seem overstated to attract attention to his blog. These electricity costs will undoubtedly come down as the technology evolves. The crypto industry should try to reduce electricity consumption, for sure; but to call it an "environmental disaster" is disingenuous and must raise questions as to motive.

There is another aspect of the "environmentalist" claim made by Augustin Carstens: he knows why a global community of millions of people are willing to spend money for crypto transactions. He knows that people spend this money because they don't trust banks. He knows that these people are the most awake, that they see that the emperor has no clothes, and that they don't believe his lies. He knows that they are a grave danger to him and the 1%. That people are willing to spend money on supporting the crypto currency ecosystem sends a tangible message, backed by their own money: we don't believe in the fractional reserve banking system and we are going to create a better world, rather than just continuing to be taken advantage of by a system that favours the 1%.

Augustin Carstens's reason for preferring the fractional reserve banking system is because ...

*"Central banks are trusted, and that trust is something they have built up over decades and for which there is no substitute right now."*

Further, *"In my experience, it is always the poorest who suffer the most from inflation. It is therefore the duty of central bankers to ensure that purchasing power is maintained."*

In addition, crypto currencies, he says, are not "*suitable as a store of value.*"

I know what you are probably thinking: gosh, maybe I should transfer my wealth into Mexican pesos, for safekeeping. I can put my trust in the Central Bank of Mexico. Before you do that, however, take a look at the chart below.

### The Mexican peso: the ultimate store of value.

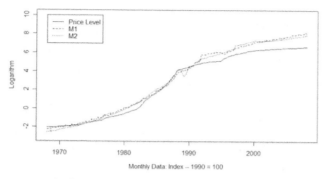

Money and Inflation: Mexico. Source: John E. Floyd, University of Toronto.

If you turn it upside down, you will see the decline in the purchasing power of the peso. Take a closer look at the y-axis. That is right: it is a log scale. For those of you who are not so mathematically minded, when your purchasing power is declining at a logarithmic rate, that is bad. The only thing that Augustin Carstens' institution has built up over decades is a logarithmic destruction in the quality of life for the Mexican people.

So, why exactly are crypto currencies not money? *"They cannot assume the functions of money for the simple reason of how they are created." "It's a fallacy to think money can be created from nothing."*

There you go: the big lie strategy again. It is so duplicitous that it is hard to believe that this comes out of his mouth. This from a man who, himself personally, has created an astronomical amount of paper money while head of the central bank in Mexico. From nothing. With his own hands. And, who knows perfectly well that his commercial bank friends create an obscene amount of their own credit money, mainly for the benefit of the Mexican 1%.

Augustin Carstens also criticises the crypto system as being used for money laundering. This from a man who oversaw the Mexican economy and central bank during a period when US authorities accuse Mexican-based banks of laundering more money from more murderous drug cartels than anywhere else, at any other time in human history.

Isn't it sweet that he references the poor, who suffer the most? Here is some more of the interview. *"Mr Carstens, how are you liking it in Basel?" "I already knew the city before I moved here. Over the past eight years, as head of the*

*Mexican central bank, I had been to Basel over 40 times* [for BIS meetings]. ... *For example, we went to Art Basel, and we've been to the old town to enjoy the Rhine. Unfortunately, we haven't made it to the zoo, though, as our dogs are not allowed in."*

That really is sad, isn't it? But, there you have it: Augustin Carstens has his problems in life, too. He is just like many of his fellow Mexicans, struggling to get by.

He has one last thing to say: *"So, my message to young people would be: Stop trying to create money!"*

It is fitting, final, inspiring words to the next generation, to those who want to make the world a better place, from a lackey of the 1%.

What he means is, *"I can create money. My friends at the banks can create money. But, don't you dare try to do it, young people. Know your place in life."*

**Takeaways**

1. Expect the 1% and their supporters to fight unfairly to defend their interests.
2. Economically speaking, Basel, Switzerland, is the darkest place on Earth.
3. Listening to Augustin Carstens denigrate young people and defend the 1% and fractional reserve banking can make you so irritated that you might consider taking up communism.
4. Supporting the crypto system might be a better alternative, to reduce inequality in society and make the world a better place.

# 16
# EIGHT PREDICTIONS FOR THE FUTURE OF THE 1% AND THEIR MONEY SYSTEM

**1. A new banking model will emerge, in accordance with our better human values.**

This model will be driven by technology and based on the concepts of user control of their account, transparency, and genuine money. Real PV money tied to real value created. With no double spending or "fractional" anything possible. Honest money for people who value freedom and fairness and who want to make better lives for themselves, without the 1% taking a cut of their labour. For people who are sick of the inherent dishonesty of the old system, its poor economic results, and its harmful impact on society.

This banking model will enable holders of crypto currencies to lend to borrowers in the real economy, in a more secure manner than currently offered by government deposit "insurance". It will allow savers to benefit from productive economic opportunities and earn a much higher return on their savings than currently possible. The deposit - borrowing dynamic is the core of banking and necessary for any currency to achieve mass adoption. Once this banking piece of the puzzle is in place it will facilitate the financial depth necessary for the crypto system to be a replacement option to the fractional reserve banking system that runs on credit money and nation state currencies.

In addition, this new banking model will allow the unbundling of banking products and services. With the traditional system, the bank mainly determines how "banking" looks to customers, regardless of whether these customers are individuals or institutions. In the future, customers will choose what they want from banking, in much the same way as customers can unbundle and then rebundle what music they want to listen to.

A key difference between the crypto system and the traditional financial system is this: the traditional system is like *analog* technology, with all of its drawbacks. The crypto system is like *digital* technology; its potential provides a base for future innovation that is hard to imagine today.

As this new banking model emerges, the power of the 1% and their influence on society will decline. As the new model will allow savers in the 99% to tap into a much higher level of economic participation in the economy, previously captured by the big banks and the 1%, economic inequality will reduce over time. This technology-based banking system will also reduce the impact of human biases in the lending decision as well as the general role of the 1%, lessening economic discrimination against out- groups in the financial system.

## 2. Fractional reserve banking will be reformed.

The government charter to commercial banks that allows them to create credit money will become regulated. Credit money creation will be subject to regulatory limits.

The free government deposit guarantee to commercial banks, which encourages speculation on future asset prices and is the cause of economic booms and busts, will be reformed. In the future, banks will have to pay for deposit insurance. Loans to finance asset purchases or for proprietary activities will be required to be capitalised separately; banks will no longer be able to use customer deposits + free government insurance to finance these activities.

## 3. But it won't matter: the fractional reserve banking system will almost completely die out over the next decade.

The crypto system will offer higher returns for less risk and depositors will increasingly vote with their feet. The two systems will co-exist for a while. Over the next decade, the crypto system will expand and the fractional reserve system will decline. An inflection point will be reached where the rate of change for both accelerates rapidly. The fractional reserve system is intrinsically structured like an inverted house of cards. There will not be some gradual decline into nothingness. Once enough deposits are taken of the bottom, the house will collapse.

That inflection point will be caused by adoption of this new banking technology. There will be four main groups that drive adoption, as set out below.

*Institutional savers in rich countries.* These include assets managers, private banks (that don't lend money), family offices, etc. They are motivated by preserving purchasing power and making a better return on their money than they get with traditional banks.

*Global commodity trade and supply chain ecosystems.* They will adopt a global standard of value as a price reference and will also be early implementers of blockchain technology to enhance their business relations, perhaps driven by the crypto banks that will emerge. Importantly, they will increasingly be willing to use crypto currencies in their borrowings, starting with small amounts, like 5-10% of the total amount. This will contribute to crypto deposits, as these accounts can be linked to interest-bearing loans that are also denominated in crypto. Some of these amounts will be hedged. This link to real economy borrowing in crypto will contribute significantly to the growth of genuine crypto banking, creating a virtuous adoption cycle.

*Individuals in emerging countries.* These are people outside of the traditional banking system, who would benefit from the superior transfer and deposit features offered by the crypto system. The financial inclusion of these people is not a charity: it is a positive economic benefit to them and their societies. They will spread adoption mainly by using mobile phones and the simple user interfaces that will emerge, regardless of national boundaries. They are not the same as the traditionally unbanked; they will participate in a new crypto banking model.

*Developing countries.* Eventually developing countries that have weak currencies will adopt the crypto system, similar to those that have become "dollarised". For a while it will exist side by side with the traditional system and people will have a choice. Eventually, most will prefer the crypto system for its superior qualities, like preservation of purchasing power, low costs, transparency, global acceptance, etc. Adoption of the crypto system will unlock economic potential for these countries, creating a positive feedback loop: as economic output increases, savings rates increase, and enabler friction is reduced, citizens will demand more of the crypto system and politicians will reap some of the benefits. Other countries will be encouraged to follow the earlier adopters. Global productivity will increase, starting first with inter-linked, international commodity trade and supply chain systems. The lives of the poor in these developing countries will improve as they are able to access a genuine savings function. Human migration and "brain-drains" will be reduced as economic equality spreads.

**4.** **International trade will increasingly be priced in a standard of value that is global and not tied to the currency of any particular country.**

The US dollar will slowly decline as a standard of value in trade. It will be replaced by the Special Drawing Rights basket (USD, EUR, GBP, JPY, CNY) + BTC. The SDR+ would just be a standard of value that would be intended to be more price stable and separate from the currency valuation actions of a single nation state. The components of this SDR+ standard of value will rebalance over time, with the role of BTC increasing and perhaps other crypto currencies being added. Exchanges can then be made in a separate currency; for example, a coffee supply transaction could be negotiated directly by a seller and a buyer with the price agreed in SDR+. On final delivery, the buyer could pay in a currency of their choice, as long as it matched the value set in SDR+. Eventually, a global standard of value may emerge for pricing that may separate from the SDR+ and simply be based on price stability, rebalancing perhaps with changes in inflation (CPI) and population.

**5.** **With greater adoption of the crypto system, variance in the economic cycles will become less extreme.**

The crypto system will reduce business cycle variance in two ways:

a.  Through the elimination of credit money creation by banks. Crypto money supply is fixed; money cannot be arbitrarily created in this system.

b.  By endowing money ownership rights in its proper holders: those who created the value in the first place. The distributed nature of the crypto system and individual control of their money allows the lending mechanism to tap into the diffusion of knowledge in society. So, since it is your money (not the bank's money) and since you have a say (as opposed to some loan officer making the decision about how "your" money should be lent). The community of savers will be properly incentivised to be more prudent when evaluating lending to asset purchases.

## 6. The future "unwinding" of money created over the past decade will lead to an accelerated decline of nation state currencies over the next decade and drive savers to adopt crypto currencies.

The unbounded money creation of the past decade, to bail-out the 1% and the fractional reserve banking system from asset mal investment, is historically unprecedented. Foresighted savers, particularly asset managers in advanced economies, will seek value preservation in the crypto system at a level greatly in excess of today's levels. When the inverted house of cards collapses again, you don't want to be holding traditional nation state currencies.

The unwinding of central bank balance sheets is guaranteed to lead to a loss of purchasing power for nation state currencies. Oh, and keep in mind that central bank money is a minority of money in the economy. The situation with commercial banks is worse.

## 7. Low income people everywhere will do their banking using the crypto system.

The fractional reserve banking system has completely failed low income people. Of course, most poor people are not even accepted by these banks. The crypto system allows everyone to benefit from financial inclusion. The poor will be able to make transfers at extremely low cost. Emerging crypto banks will allow them the benefits of the savings function, giving them the first opportunity ever to climb out of poverty. The effects for poor communities globally will be *transformational*.

Here is a typical example of how the 1% treats those poor people who are fortunate enough even to have bank accounts, from one of Warren Buffett's top investments:

## 8. Micro-everything will explode in use.

The crypto system allows extremely small amounts of money to be used in the financial system. For example, transfers for only a few dollars equivalent can be made. Emerging crypto banks will allow savers to put very small amounts of value to work, on which people can earn interest.

The poor will be able to hold just a few satoshis worth of global stocks or bonds. Even the yield curve will be able to be constructed on a micro-level, for example the lending function could happen based on a day basis, rather than on wide fixed dates with interpolation between such dates for pricing in the credit markets at the moment. It will *revolutionise* finance.

These are problems for which the only technology solution is the crypto system. As in so many improvements, the traditional banking system simply cannot offer such solutions; they are stuck in an outdated, analog world.

### Takeaways

1.  The best way to challenge the influence of the 1% on society, moderate excesses in the business cycle, and reduce inequality is to address the money creation power of banks.
2.  Technology offers the possibility of an alternative money system that is superior to today's system.
3.  By adopting this technology, we have the potential to mitigate some of these negative aspects of the current system.
4.  Our choice will be as much about our values as it is about the technicalities of the two systems.

# 17
# THE CHOICE TODAY

Previous great generations had their own battles to fight, whether it was against totalitarian ideologies, against racism, or against sexism. The battle for our generation will be partly against the inequality personified in the 1% and their dishonest, discriminatory banking system. A system that, in the best case, holds us back from living life to the fullest or, in the worst case, excludes us because we are an out-group. A system that disadvantages the many to benefit the few. A system that preys on our ignorance in order to survive. A system that underpins much of the moral rottenness in other areas of life.

If you want to do some field research, to compare the two systems, go find the Filipino maid standing in line at some foreign exchange bureau. The one who sells herself into slavery to support a daughter back home. So, at least the daughter might have the hope of a better future. Tap the maid on the shoulder and ask how much our modern financial system is going to take from her earnings. 10%? 20%? 30%?

What would she get her daughter if she had this extra money? More food? Better clothes? Music lessons? How many years, how much less time away from her daughter would this extra money bring her? And, what interest rate is she getting on her savings in her bank account? Does a bank even give her an account? Probably not.

You tell her that a new system is coming. In this new system, the money she worked hard for belongs to her, not to the bank. A system where sending money to someone will be quick and cheap, like sending information. You tell her that, in the 21st century, we will endure this old system no longer.

And what about you? What would you do with the extra money you would earn on your bank deposit, if the 1% and their system didn't take most of the margins? Technology has transformed almost all industries over the past generation. Only core banking, deposits and loans, remain virtually untouched. Only in this industry do you find large and growing profits, shielded from competition by their enablers, the machine that feeds the 1% and casts a malignant shadow over society.

Money is fundamental to life; it is how we keep track of much of our productive effort and how we care for others. It is not simply a question of one technology against another; it is a question of our values. Our choices in the future, whether we continue to lend our money to the 1%'s banking system or not, will speak to the character of our generation.

In this fight, like all great struggles, despite the odds, we must believe that the human desire for freedom and fairness will prevail.

In this fight, you are either with a community that aspires to make the world a better place, or you are with the big banks.

In this fight, you are either the idealism personified by Satoshi Nakamoto or you are Augustin Carstens.

# 18
# CONCLUSION

*A defining feature of the 1% is their preferential access to money and their relationship with the banking sector.*

The term "1%" is used here as a shorthand for elites, the establishment. Of course, the 1% are not a monolithic group and there is a wide range of factors that characterise any such body of people. However, their actions exhibit notable commonality of interests. This is particularly evident during periods of financial dislocation.

The banking system, and the "money" that it produces, is intrinsically based on dishonesty and deception. It is simply a fact that fractional reserve banking involves an untruth at its core: the depositor is told that their money is safely held in the bank while, at the same time, the bank lends most of this money to borrowers or uses it for its own purposes. Similarly, the banking process involves a number of misrepresentations, including: that depositors are told that the money in the bank belongs to them when, legally, it is an unsecured loan from them to the bank; that the "deposit" is insured when, in fact, there is no insurance fund whatsoever, etc. Little details like that.

The structure of the fractional reserve banking system essentially facilitates wealth transfer over time, from the majority to a small minority, contributing to inequality in society. Savers are vastly undercompensated  for their contribution to bank profits and for the risk they assume by making deposits (lending, actually) in banks. Banks are best evaluated using real option pricing theory and the input parameters described in this book.

Consequently, the accumulation of wealth by the banking sector (and the 1%) mimics a series of games with asymmetrical risk-reward characteristics, where profits are captured by the 1% and losses are borne by everyone in society. As an analogy, many people can probably relate to the experience of playing the board game Monopoly. As each player takes turns, it emerges that one player increasingly accumulates the majority of the wealth in the game until they win, although this may take some time. To compare this to the advantages enjoyed by the 1%, imagine playing Monopoly where one of the players has access to money on more advantageous terms than the rest and never has any downside. Any losses are paid for by all players. But, when that player has a success, the player keeps all of the rewards. And yeah, that player gets to be the banker. You think such an arrangement might encourage some risk-taking? Don't really like the idea of playing a game with this kind of rules? Well, I have news for you: you are playing it right now. In real life. *This is what they don't want you to know.*

Member of an out-group? Well, access to money is always going to be harder for you; it is an intrinsic part of the risk evaluation process in fractional reserve banking. Humans have inherent biases and, when bankers are creating assets (and the concomitant "money"), they are aware of the inverted house of cards structure above them. They are very focused on expected, risk-adjusted cashflows and are very sensitive to "g". The end result is that in creating assets - FV money they are naturally going to find groups with similarities less risky. They are making these decisions with the interest of a principal, an investment company mainly investing their own money, not just as some financial intermediary.

In addition, the 1%'s banking system is largely responsible for the excess variance in the business cycle. While there will likely always be some degree of variance to the cycle, the presence of bank-created money amplifies the effect materially. This presents a danger for society, similar to rising inequality. The use of bank-created money for financing asset purchases is the cause of most booms and busts in the economy. Neither banks' creation of money nor the use of funds is regulated at all. A bank's own, internally created, credit money makes up most of the sources of funds for the loans that it makes; funds influenced by the central bank price of money are a minority of its sources. For this reason, central bank monetary policy is an ineffective tool for controlling the excess variance in the economic cycle.

This book is written for a general audience and does not pretend to present an academic case study. Certainly, this could be done and published in an economics journal and it is unlikely that more than handful of people would read it. That wasn't my objective.

Maybe better than an academic study would be to put the problem to Homer Simpson. You could say, well, the punch bowl keeps going in and out and we keep gazing into our crystal balls and the economy still experiences booms and busts just like it has for hundreds of years. Since the creation of the Fed, we are now at 19 recessions and counting. Do you think that this model works very well? Or, under our banking system, when cashflows from assets are positive, the banks and the 1% keep the profits; when they don't work out, all of us absorb the losses. Do you think that if we keep doing this over time that wealth will be transferred from the many to the few? "Duh", he would probably say.

The takeaways are clear:

Banks create most of the money in the economy, not the state. They use this money to advance their own objectives.

The 1% get a meaningful part of their power from their relationship with the banking system, which contributes to their influence in society.

Inequality arises from the unjustified margins captured by the banks; from risk evaluation biases, exacerbated by the pressures of the inverted house of cards structure of fractional reserve banking; and from the accumulated benefits of the asymmetric profit pay-offs inherent in the system.

Wealth capture by the 1% has been increasing for the past several generations, as the financial sector grows in size at a faster rate than the overall economy. At the same time, lower and middle class incomes and opportunities have declined.

Central bank monetary policy ignores the fact that banks create their own money and has almost no effect on moderating booms and busts in the business cycle, leaving society exposed to bank-caused economic downturns.

Addressing the issues caused by bank money creation isn't a question of raising taxes (which the 1% can mostly find ways around anyway) or after-the-fact government intervention; it is a structural question about the wealth transfer mechanism inherent in the fractional reserve banking system and the effect on the economic cycle of using bank-created money for asset purchases.

Addressing these issues also isn't a question of left or right in politics; it should be of bi-partisan interest. The 1% and the fractional reserve banking system disadvantage everyone, regardless of their political affiliation.

Thanks for taking the time to read the book. I hope that you now have a better understanding of money, how banks really function, and their impact on society. I also hope that the book has cleared up some (economic) mysteries for you.

Now is the time to take a stand for what you believe in, Robert.

# ABOUT THE AUTHOR

Robert Sharratt is part-Canadian, part-British, somewhat autistic and lives in Geneva. He is going to create a better banking model, or die trying. His interests include mountain-climbing, chess, piano, programming and distrusting authority. In his early career, he was an M&A investment banker in London, then in private equity, and then moved to Switzerland to invest his own money. He holds an MSc degree in Finance from London Business School.


Medium: @res_crescofin
Twitter: @res_crescofin


Pronunciation: Sharratt -> like "share it"